CAN GOVERNMENTS LEARN?

Comparative Policy Analysis Series
Ray C. Rist, Series Editor

Budgeting, Auditing, and Evaluation,
edited by Andrew Gray, Bill Jenkins, and Bob Segsworth

Can Governments Learn?
edited by Frans L. Leeuw, Ray C. Rist, and Richard C. Sonnichsen

Program Evaluation and the Management of Government,
edited by Ray C. Rist

CAN GOVERNMENTS LEARN?

Comparative Perspectives on Evaluation & Organizational Learning

Edited by
Frans L. Leeuw, Ray C. Rist & Richard C. Sonnichsen

Transaction Publishers
New Brunswick (U.S.A.) and London (U.K.)

Copyright © 1994 by Transaction Publishers,
New Brunswick, New Jersey 08903

All rights reserved under International and Pan-American Copyright Conventions. No part of this book may be reproduced or transmitted in any form or by any means, electronic or mechanical, including photocopy, recording, or any information storage and retrieval system, without prior permission in writing from the publisher. All inquiries should be addressed to Transaction Publishers, Rutgers—The State University, New Brunswick, New Jersey 08903.

Library of Congress Catalog Number: 93-24956
ISBN: 1-56000-130-5 (cloth)
Printed in the United States of America

Library of Congress Cataloging-in-Publication Data

Can governments learn? : comparative perspectives on evaluation and organizational learning / [edited by] Frans L. Leeuw, Ray C. Rist, Richard C. Sonnichsen.
    p.   cm.
Includes bibliographical references and index.
ISBN 1-56000-130-5
1. Public administration—Evaluation—Case studies.
2. Organizational behavior—Evaluation—Case studies.
3. Organizational change—Evaluation—Case studies. I. Leeuw, Frans L. II. Rist, Ray C. III. Sonnichsen, Richard C.
JF1411.C24   1993
350.007'6—dc20   93-24956
                                                               CIP

For Bjarne Eriksen—

*Friend, Colleague, and Founding Member of the
IIAS Working Group on Policy and Program Evaluation*

Contents

Introduction: Evaluations and Organizational Learning:
International Perspectives
   Frans L. Leeuw and Richard C. Sonnichsen   1

Part I   National Perspectives

1. Utilizing Evaluation in Organizations: The Balancing Act
   John Mayne (Canada)   17

2. Learning from Evaluations: The Swedish Experience
   Jan-Eric Furubo (Sweden)   45

3. Policy Evaluation and the Netherlands's Government:
Scope, Utilization, and Organizational Learning
   Frans L. Leeuw and Piet J. Rozendal (The Netherlands)   67

Part II   Institutional Perspectives

4. Organizational Learning at the U.S. Office of Personnel
Management
   John A. Leitch and Ray C. Rist (United States)   89

5. Formative Evaluation and Organizational Learning:
The Case of the Belgium Postal System
   Philippe Spaey and Fabienne Leloup (Belgium)   107

6. Effective Internal Evaluation: An Approach
to Organizational Learning
   Richard C. Sonnichsen (United States)   125

Part III When Do Governments Learn?

7 Facilitating Organizational Learning: Human Resource
     Management and Program Evaluation
   Marie Louise Bemelmans-Videc (The Netherlands)
   Bjarne Eriksen (Norway)
   Edie N. Goldenberg (United States)   145

8 The Preconditions for Learning:
     Lessons from the Public Sector
   Ray C. Rist (United States)   189

Contributors   207

Index   211

Introduction

Evaluation and Organizational Learning: International Perspectives

Frans L. Leeuw and Richard C. Sonnichsen

In the original scheme of things, the individual policymaker was viewed as a rational actor who needed more and better information to make more and better decisions. The decision maker was portrayed as a thoughtful person who could be convinced by evidence and who would make sound judgments based on the merits of available knowledge. This knowledge directly shaped decision making, which led directly to action. The relation of information to action was presumed to be linear and straightforward. Yet, during the early conceptualization of the ways in which program evaluation might be used as a tool for organizational improvement, there was little to no attention paid to theoretical understandings of organizational learning processes or the manner in which organizations assimilated and used information.

As the years have passed and the research into knowledge utilization has grown considerably, the evidence now suggests that this linear assumption is naive—it is naive for any given individual and it is naive for an organization. The incorporation of information into the knowledge base of an individual or an organization is selective, sporadic, and temporal. And beyond that, decisionmaking takes place in a context where "rational information" is but one among many contending forces.

Besides reconceptualizing the linear concept of knowledge acquisition by organizations, organizational theorists have begun to portray organizations as deficient at in-depth probing of the assumptions that drive their administrative and operational policies. Historically, organizations have not been thought to be effective at identifying the root causes that generate their problems. They are often described as limiting themselves to "tinkering at the margins" when confronted with a problem or crisis.

This approach to organizational problem solving ensures the recurrence of similar problems since the basic cause has been neither identified nor addressed. In other words, organizations are not always good learners. Organizational learning is usually not a deliberate enterprise, but an ad hoc endeavor used for problem solving. This approach results in an residual buildup of rules, policies, traditions, and cultural artifacts that affect the decision-making process and constrain the decision maker. Further, numerous entities within an organization often compete in the production of information, each with their own biases, agendas, and objectives. Often a parochial perspective (read "self-interest") dominates these viewpoints.

Organizational Learning: The Theoretical Underpinnings

Argyris (1982) argues that organizations have great difficulty in learning and seldom question the underlying basis of their own problems. Organizations have been depicted as lacking in innovation and intrinsically resistant to change, stressing conformity instead of creativity. Some theorists challenged organizations to develop more adaptive structures for problem solving (Thompson 1969; Bennis 1971). For organizations to learn, develop, and grow they require the acquisition of knowledge (Dery 1986); however, organizations are incapable of acquiring and digesting all available information. Therefore, selective acquisition and discarding takes place. This accretion of knowledge is dependent on the capacity for learning, that is, rigorously examining on a recurring basis organizational actions and reasoning processes. Self-inspection is but one effective tool that can be employed for organizations to discover and correct deficiencies, adjust activities, and alter operational tasks to ensure effective and efficient goal attainment.

Argyris (1982) defines organizational learning as a "process of detecting and correcting error." It is a process in which an organization continually attempts to become competent in taking action, while at the same time reflecting on the action it takes to learn from its present and past efforts. The organizational learning process, as depicted by Argyris, is an iterative process of applying assimilated knowledge to solve organizational problems. His conceptual approach differentiates learning as occurring in either a single or double loop mode. Problem solving that enables an organization to better carry out its present policies and achieve its current objectives is defined as "single-loop learning." A more comprehensive and systemic learning process occurs when "double-loop learning" occurs. In this case the assumptions underlying the policies and goals of a program are questioned, leading to the possibility of securing new and innovative permanent solutions to problems.

Single-loop learning occurs when individuals detect a match or mismatch of outcomes to organizational expectations. In the instance of a match, current policies and procedures are likely left as they are. When there is a mismatch, however, the organization strives to realign outcomes within organizational expectations without questioning the underlying causal mechanisms that precipitated the problem. Error detection is necessary for error correction.

A double-loop learning environment encourages the questioning of assumptions and confronting of the traditions in an organization that are being advocated. In this learning system, people advocate their views in such a way that would invite confrontation so that their positions might be challenged in a public forum. In other words, the underlying assumptions, norms, and objectives that pertain to the problem under discussion would be open to confrontation. That can also be the case with regard to assumptions underlying the selected policy programs, instruments, or organizational structures aimed at the reduction of the problems encountered. Studies published by Mason and Mitroff (1981), Chen (1990), and Leeuw (1985; 1991) have stressed ways to reconstruct these "theories-in-use" and then evaluate them.

Double-loop learning always requires an opposition of ideas for comparison: learning occurs when the underlying policies, norms, theories, and objectives of the organization are questioned. This approach to learning is difficult since it demands that organizations function in a continual questioning mode with contesting views of operations. If fully implemented, this would approach Wildavsky's (1979) "self-evaluating" organization.

Although many contemporary organizational problems are double-loop in nature, Argyris argues that they are usually approached within a single-loop perspective. This occurs since people are reluctant to question underlying policies and values in an organization and shy away from confronting threatening issues. Candid questioning of an organizational policy can create difficult and complex group dynamics that many persons will actively try to avoid. Argyris labels this avoidance of personal responsibility for solving problems, "distancing."

Evaluation as an Aid to Organizational Learning

Organizational learning requires an exchange of information between the organization and both its internal and external environments. The exchange allows the organization to monitor these environments and initiate responses accordingly. For such exchange to occur, four conditions have to be met. First, the organization must have the capacity to sense, monitor, and scan significant aspects of its internal and external environments. Second, it must be able to relate this information to the organization's operating norms and values that guide the organization and which may be inferred from its directly observable behavior. Third, it must be able to detect significant deviation from the norms or procedures that it follows so that, fourth, it can initiate appropriate action to correct any deficiencies.

Now it must be stressed that evaluation research is only *one* of the feedback mechanisms capable of stimulating single- or double-loop learning. Investigative journalism, for example, is an other mechanism, as is the case with regard to "sabbatical leaves" of senior management within an organization, where their time away is focused on in-depth reviewing of the organizational goals and programs. However, we stress the specific importance of evaluations as an important feedback mechanism to an organization and we do so for two reasons.

First, evaluation research can be characterized by adhering to meth-

Introduction 5

odological standards of robustness, validity, and reliability and is a compelling force of truth (Arendt 1969). And second, this type of social policy research can be linked to the necessity of discharging the public responsibility of intervening in society. James Coleman (1990: 623) has written in this regard:

> The growth in social policy research did not begin until the major shift in claims and responsibilities in the 1960's. It was the social policies of the 1950's, 1960's and 1970's that stimulated social policy research. The reasons why the growth of national social policy generated social policy research are several but it is sufficient to note one: As the national government assumed public responsibility in matters where responsibility had been local and private, it was ill-equipped to discharge this responsibility. ... Research was necessary to learn how a social welfare program should be modified, whether it should be continued, even whether it was working in the manner intended. *Because social policy was enacted at a national level and its execution occurred at a local level, the old, direct, informal methods of getting such feedback were no longer effective.* (Emphasis added)

Feedback to organizations after error detection, for the subsequent purpose of correcting what is wrong, is what much of program evaluation by intent is all about. Whether the terms are "process evaluation," "formative evaluation," "program monitoring," or "economy and efficiency audits," the intent is the same: Find out what is going on so that responsible decision makers can make the necessary corrections and modifications to keep the program on track.

When an organization connects the information that comes from its detection efforts to strategies and assumptions for effective performance within existing standard operating procedures, it is practicing single-loop learning. But if it uses that information to examine basic assumptions about the norms and standards for the organization or policy itself, then double-loop learning occurs. This capacity to routinely examine the basic assumptions behind organizational procedures and test their appropriateness requires an organization with a high degree of rationality and maturity. It must be able to monitor itself, initiate appropriate changes, and then study those changes to see if they were or were not effective. Double-loop learning, says Argyris, requires an "organizational inquiry which resolves incompatible organizational norms by setting new priorities and weightings of norms, or by restructuring the norms themselves together with associated strategies and assumptions."

It should be noted that policies and goals set by organizations are all part of the organizational culture. The development towards openness to change and innovation, which is essential in organizational learning, can be sustained by a longer-term belief in the necessity of change. To that effect, the organizational culture will need to allow for competition between various views and perspectives. Here, for example, an organization's human resources policy can have a profound impact on the organizational learning process. (See the more detailed discussion of this point in a later chapter of this book by Bemelmans-Videc et al.)

As mentioned earlier, many—or rather most—evaluations have been designed to help the policymaker at becoming more proficient in single-loop learning. Evaluations are designed to help the organization monitor its performance in relation to the objectives set for the policy or program. Evaluations are central to the persistent question of any organization: "How well are we doing?" There is evidence that some evaluations have been conducted that would allow the evaluator to enter into substantial dialogue (i.e., double-loop learning) with the policymaker. There are a number of documented instances of this dialogue in the subsequent chapters of this book.

Policy Process, Evaluation, and Learning

Till now, we have not distinguished between types of organizational learning on the one hand and characteristics of policy processes on the other hand. Neither have we been giving much attention to illustrations of what in practice is meant by single- and double-loop learning. Focusing on two characteristics of the policy process, which Chelimsky distinguished, we will be more specific now. She (1985: 8) has written:

> Decision-makers may need information from evaluation for (several) very broad kinds of purposes: for policy execution—that is, to ensure that a program is implemented in the most cost-effective way; and for accountability in public decision making—that is, to determine the effectiveness of an operating program and the need for its continuation, modification or termination.

The following hypothetical illustrations of single- and double-loop learning in the field of a nation's policy for refugee education can be mentioned. We are assuming the presence of evaluation research dealing with this refugee policy. The research has focused on the impact of training programs in special institutions, spread out over a country. It has been shown via previous evaluations that the curricula of these schools and the ways of selecting refugees to attend these schools are not at all adequate and efficient. When these results are used by (among others) the Ministry of Refugee Affairs, regional and state administrators, and school councils, and when the use indicates that these organizations are planning to change certain elements of the curricula as well as the selection and admission procedures, then single-loop learning with regard to the formulation of this policy has occurred.

Double-loop learning will occur in a different way. Assume again evaluation research on the relationship between, on the one hand, the geographically dispersed "special school-system" for refugees and, on the other hand, the goal-achievement of the refugee policy. Assume also that evaluations have shown that the level of goal achievement is very limited, while the implementation of the policy has been adequate. This makes clear that the very idea of special refugee schools is not effective. When these findings are used by the aforementioned actors/stakeholders, for example by setting up a working committee with the task to develop a strategy for the de-institutionalization of the refugee training and school system, and when, subsequently, the conclusions of this committee lead to new ideas and suggestions about how to accommodate and integrate refugees (for example by closing these special schools), then double-loop learning with regard to policy formulation has occurred.

Now we go over to the relationship between organizational learning and accountability, which is the other element Chelimsky (1985) mentioned. Assume once again the presence of evaluation research dealing with the refugee education policy. The evaluation has shown that the curricula of the schools and the ways of selecting refugees are inadequate in terms of performance indicators applied. When these results are used by the Ministry of Refugee Affairs to change technical elements of the performance indicators, then single-loop learning with regard to the aspect of "accountability" has occurred. However, when the evaluations have shown that the level of goal-achievement is limited and when these findings lead to a fundamental reconsideration of the complete system of performance indicators as well as of their underlying assumptions, then double-loop learning has occurred.

Organizational Integration of Evaluations

Accepting the conceptual framework that evaluation can benefit organizations by assisting in the problem-solving process does not obviate the pragmatic side of evaluation practice. In order to play a systematic role in the decision-making process from either the viewpoint of single-loop or double-loop learning, more than the proper design and executing of an evaluation are needed. Design and execution are mainly technical aspects of evaluations. The argument that organizations are inadequate at developing the capacity for double-loop learning and that evaluation is an intervention capable of enhancing such capacity requires an examining of the integration of evaluation into the organizational administrative process.

Rist (1990) has made the useful distinction between management *of* evaluations and management *by* evaluations. In his view, the managerial input into the evaluation effort has considerable influence on the evaluation outcomes. In order to integrate the evaluation function with policy processes in governmental organizations, the evaluation function has to be constructively managed. Rist identifies the degree of independence that characterizes evaluation units, the dissemination of evaluation reports, and the organizational structures and systems as the essential elements necessary to perform effective policy evaluations.

To ensure that policy and program evaluation play a systematic instead of an ad hoc role in the process of organizational learning, an environment should be created that encourages the efficient and timely performance of evaluations as well as the utilization of their results. This implies that a certain level of institutionalization has to occur before evaluations can play a role in the management of government organizations. Derlien (1990) believes that unless conducting evaluation studies becomes institutionalized, their occurrence and then certainly their use tends to be random.

Institutionalization is important irrespective of whether evaluations are performed by internal or external evaluators. Derlien focuses on adequate administration, quality control, and financial ramifications pertaining to external evaluation studies. Hoogerwerf and Zoutendijk (1991) have enumerated a series of organizational arrangements and procedures that together shape the "evaluation structure." These authors explain the necessity of using contracts when evaluations are carried out by external investigators, suggest adequate ways of diffusing and archiving results of evaluation projects, and the handling of available time and financial budgets. Hoogerwerf and Zoutendijk also suggest that within larger governmental organizations, one or more specific units should deal with the development and maintenance of this infrastructure.

Finally, it should be stressed that institutionalization can in the end only be prolonged in terms of a mutual affirmation of structure and culture within an organization. One of the ways to shed light on this is to look at policies of organizations that deal with human resources management and this is exactly the focus of the Bemelmans-Videc et al. chapter to come later in this volume.

Conclusions

The underlying premise of this book is that although organizational learning can come from many sources, evaluations can contribute strongly to the organizational learning process. The purpose of our research is to identify those instances where evaluations have contributed to major policy examination and positive change. We have also sought to determine the characteristics of the evaluations and the organizational conditions that existed and allowed the learning process to occur. Our hypothesis is twofold. The first part concerns the proper design of evaluation: evaluations precipitate debate on core organizational issues when they not only ask the question "how well are we doing," but also, "does it make sense to do it, even if it is being done well?" The second part of the hypothesis concerns the element of institutionalization: properly designed evaluations will stimulate the occurrence of such debates when they are adequately managed by the organization.

The fundamental and profound changes required of organizations who engage in double-loop learning are difficult, time consuming, and risky. Few positive incentives exist for program personnel to embark on an uncertain examination of core program issues with potentially negative unintended consequences. Evaluation offices, however, are significantly less encumbered than program personnel. If they are asked to perform independent and critical reviews of programs, they can offer organizations an effective mechanism to examine program activities, underlying assumptions, and offer recommendations for alternative strategies. Program evaluation, however, cannot be characterized as a panacea for organizational learning since it is but one of numerous competing approaches to collecting and furnishing data to decision makers.

The purpose of this book is to explore some of the political and organizational conditions encountered by evaluators in Western countries that are relevant with regard to the use made of evaluations in contributing to the organizational learning process. Evaluators, functioning as conduits of information from the inside of programs to top government and organizational officials, can increase the quality of the decision-making process and help organizations toward single- and double-loop learning.

The linkage between evaluation and organizational learning is occasionally causal, but generally difficult to establish since evaluation is but one of numerous competing entities. Evaluation results are seldom the only data applied to and used in the decision-making process. Properly designed and managed evaluations, however, offer the decisionmaker insights from an impartial perspective since the evaluators have no stake in the outcome. Evaluators, operating in a double-loop mode examining core organizational issues, also have the potential to provide an empirical basis for the debate on major organizational policies.

Perhaps two-thirds of the evaluation examples in this volume can be characterized as single-loop learning. The remaining studies have described instances where evaluation was used to generate double-loop learning. But regardless of type, these studies show that evaluation can be an effective analytical approach to enhance organizational learning. The end result can be the improvement of tools and programs of government through the rigorous examination of public policy and processes and the recommendation of change.

The chapters, here have taken as their point of departure the empirical question of whether (and how) evaluation studies are used by organizations. The term *used* is broadly framed to address not only any indications of direct impacts, but to look for indirect influences as well. The intent has been to systematically analyze conditions relevant for utilizing evaluation studies in relation to the learning processes of public sector organizations. The findings suggest that conditions differ within the respective countries, which in turn, and as one might anticipate, influence the dynamics of organizational learning.

The authors are all participants in an ongoing Working Group on Policy and Program Evaluation sponsored by the International Institute of Administrative Sciences in Brussels, Belgium. The working group is comprised of members from both government and academia.

The book consists of three parts. In Part I, attention is paid to the role policy and program evaluations play within the public sector in three different countries: Canada, the Netherlands, and Sweden. The papers also try to locate situations in which there is single- and double-loop learning as well as give insights into determinants of these situations. Mayne analyzes the current situation in Canada and grounds his findings and conclusions on documentary evidence as well as in-depth interviews with some thirty top officials in the evaluation branch of the Federal Canadian Government. As evaluation activities have been prominent in the Canadian Federal system for more than fifteen years now and as Canada has a rather well-developed organizational infrastructure, this chapter can also be seen as a review of what has been accomplished over those years.

Leeuw and Rozendal also combine a multimethod approach in their study dealing with the Netherlands. One of their questions deals with the way in which policy and program evaluation is institutionalized in this country. Another question addressed here refers to the relationships between institutionalization and utilization, and the third links both factors with three cases of learning. Jan-Eric Furubo takes the Swedish system of evaluations and audits as a point of departure, describes features of this system, and tackles the question of the extent to which findings from these activities are utilized. He also tries to link developments with regard to the budgetary process in Sweden with utilization and organizational learning. All three chapters report on empirical investigations describing developments on a macro-organizational level, and are government-wide in nature. However, they also focus on determinants of these developments on the level of single case studies.

In Part II we focus on several large-scale specific organizations and reframe the topic of evaluation, utilization and learning to a meso-organizational level, indicating that we now turn to analysis within organizations. Rist and Leitch explore an instance of double-loop learning that emerged in the U.S. Office of Personnel Management (OPM) as a result of a General Accounting Office (GAO) study. The GAO was able to document a number of gaps in the information systems used at OPM. When OPM began to address how to fill these information gaps, they soon also began asking more fundamental questions about what kinds of information they actually needed, who in the organization needed what, and how trustworthy were the present data systems. All this focus on the basic uses of information within OPM has lead to a basic re-examination of their information systems—hence the emergence of double-loop learning.

Spaey focuses on the Belgium Post Office and the ways in which evaluations play a role in the re-modeling of this organization. As the Belgium Post Office in recent years has been changed fairly dramatically (from a typical bureaucratic organization to a more client-oriented one), the information Spaey presents us is illuminating, particularly as to the role evaluation played in monitoring change at the local level.

Sonnichsen describes research conducted at internal evaluation offices in the U.S. federal government where he found examples of evaluators contributing to both single- and double-loop learning. Combining the common patterns that contributed to successful evaluation practice, Sonnichsen constructed a model of an internal evaluation office that provides a framework for evaluators who wish to influence organizations through their evaluation activities.

In the final and third part of the book, attention is shifted toward two other topics. The first concerns the educational, personnel, and cultural conditions facilitating evaluations, utilization, and organizational learning. Bemelmans-Videc et al., gathering for what we believe to be the first-time cross-national empirical data in this field, present an overview of the importance of these conditions in a number of countries, including the United States, Canada, and eight European countries. The second and final topic concerns the summarizing and comparing of the various concepts and data in the book. Rist undertakes this task and does so from the following perspective: what can be said about the relative importance of factors that facilitate both types of organizational learning and how can double-loop learning be stimulated?

References

Arendt, H. 1969. "Truth and Politics 1." In *Philosophy, Politics and Society.*, ed. P. Laslett and W.G. Runciman, 104–33. Oxford: Basil Blackwell.

Argyris, C. 1982. *Reasoning, Learning, and Action.* San Francisco: Jossey-Bass Publishers.

Bennis, W.G. 1971. "Changing Organizations." In *Social Intervention: A Behavioral Science Approach.*, ed. H.A. Hornstein, Bunker, B., Burke, W., Gindes, M., and R. Lewick; New York: Free Press.

Chelimsky, E., ed. 1985. *Program Evaluation: Patterns and Directions.* Washington, DC: American Society for Public Administration.

Chen, H.T. 1990. *Theory-Driven Evaluations.* Newbury Park, CA: Sage.

Coleman, J. 1990. *Foundations of Social Theory.* Cambridge, MA: The Bellknap Press.

Derlien, H.U. 1990. "Genesis and Structure of Evaluation Efforts in Comparative Perspective." In *Program Evaluation and the Management of Government: Patterns and Prospects across Eight Countries,* ed. Ray C. Rist, New Brunswick, NJ: Transaction Publishers.

Dery, D. 1986. "Knowledge and Organizations." *Policy Studies Review* 6, no. 1.

Hoogerwerf, A., and D.C. Zoutendijk. 1991. "Hoe valt het evaluatieonderzoek zelf te beoordelen." In *Beleidseva luatie,* ed. J. Bressers and A. Hoogerwerf, 229–47. Alphen a/d Rijn: Samson.

Leeuw, F. L. 1985. "Population Policy in Industrialized Countries: Evaluating Policy Theories." *Genus* 40: 1-23.

———. 1991. "Policy Theories, Knowledge Utilization and Evaluation." *Knowledge and Policy* 4.

Mason, R.O., and I.I. Mitroff. 1981. *Challenging Strategic Planning Assumptions.* New York: Wiley.

Rist, R. C., ed. 1990. *Program Evaluation and the Management of Government.* New Brunswick: Transaction Publishers.

Sonnichsen, R. C. 1991. "Characteristics of High Impact Internal Evaluation Offices." Ph.D. diss., University of Southern California.

Thompson, V.A. 1969. *Bureaucracy and Innovation.* Birmingham: University of Alabama Press.

Wildavsky, A. 1979. *Speaking Truth to Power: The Art and Craft of Policy Analysis.* Boston: Little, Brown and Company.

PART I

National Perspectives

1

Utilizing Evaluation in Organizations: The Balancing Act

John Mayne

> *This non-learning from patent facts—this obstinate and persistent non-learning makes me pessimistic . . . the power of blinding ourselves to patent facts seems to me almost insuperable.*
> —Arnold J. Toynbee

The extent to which findings and conclusions from evaluations of programs are used to inform decision making has received substantial attention in the literature.[1] There is considerable debate on the extent of utilization that has occurred or does occur.[2] And there are frequent laments that utilization is at best limited and considerable advice offered as to how utilization can be increased.

This chapter examines evaluation utilization in organizations, using the extensive experience gained in the Canadian federal government with evaluation units in departments. The chapter has two purposes: to present data and insight gained from evaluation practice in Canadian federal departments and agencies and to propose a conceptual supply/demand model to explain the nature and extent of evaluation utilization in organizations. The model suggests that evaluation utilization in an organization is best enhanced by evaluators proactively balancing the demand for evaluative information with its supply.

Evaluation Utilization

It is useful to distinguish between two basic types of evaluation and their use. Historically, evaluation was a component of social science research and much evaluation practice continues in this tradition. Utilization of much of this type of evaluation is often referred to as enlightenment utilization (Weiss 1977; Bulmer 1982); that is, over time the cumulative effects of scientific findings have an impact on our understanding of interventions in society and thereby affect the kinds of programs introduced to deal with social problems. Without denying the value of such research-type evaluation, it is not the subject of interest here. Rather, we are looking at evaluation that has as its aim a more immediate effect on programs,[3] what we will call "program evaluation" as opposed to "evaluation research."[4]

A program evaluation is commissioned by an organization with the aim of determining how well a program is working, and whether it needs to be improved or abandoned. Evaluation research, in contrast, is usually "commissioned" by the researcher doing the evaluation. Accumulated learning and enlightenment over time can and do occur as a result of program evaluations, as in most fields of investigation and research. But accepting this as adequate utilization in a field that is not basic research is unsatisfactory. Expectations for program evaluation are and should be much more demanding; we should aim for the performance of the program evaluated to actually improve as a result.

We are particularly interested in organizations that have an internal evaluation (Love 1991) capacity. In these cases, the organization has established a unit in the organization to undertake evaluation of its programs. The expectations for these evaluations must be program improvement, the organization expects to learn from evaluation and adapt itself accordingly. The organization has accepted, at least in part, the need to be self-evaluating (Wildavsky 1985), undertaking either single- or double-loop learning, that is, either modifying existing program operations or revising the objectives of programs.[5] While not every evaluation study need make a significant impact, over a period of time one should expect that internal evaluation has played a significant role in program improvement. Rist (1990) points out that utilization of evaluation can take place throughout the life of a program, reflecting formative, process, and outcome types of evaluation.

Utilizing Evaluation in Organizations 19

In all cases, however, the intention is still the improvement of the program. Most of the data presented later comes from process, and outcome evaluations.

It is clear that utilization of evaluations in an organization can occur in a number of ways, and there is no universally agreed typology of use. For the purpose of this chapter, utilization of program evaluations is broken down into two basic types, program use and organizational use. Program use relates to individual evaluation studies while organizational use refers to the cumulative effect on the organization of routinely carrying out evaluations over time. These terms are first defined and then discussed.

Program use (instrumental) can be defined as occurring when there is a documented instance of a specific program change made as a result of the evaluation (modifications to operations, significant reforms, or termination) or the program is explicitly confirmed as it is.

Program use (conceptual) can be defined as occurring when there is cumulative evidence that while no specific change is made in the program, still as a result of the evaluation there is better information, increased understanding of and/or better reporting on the program and its performance; in short, intellectual capital has been created.

Organizational use can be defined as occurring when there is longitudinal evidence that a cumulative effect of the evaluation function exists in the organization over time, resulting in a more results-oriented approach to management and planning, including more and better use of program performance information.

Instrumental use, as defined here, requires a specific implemented decision about the program made as a result of the evaluation.[6] It would also include changes to other programs that resulted from the specific evaluation study. In addition, it is used here to cover the case where the evaluation demonstrates that the program is working well, no (significant) improvements need be made and the program is consciously reconfirmed. Conceptual use covers the cases where, for whatever reason, decisions about the program are not forthcoming but the findings have been considered and valuable information and insight has been acquired about the specific program that is likely to be used in the future. It covers a more nebulous type of utilization and in the absence of instrumental use, most evaluations are likely to claim conceptual use. However, where possible, it is useful to distinguish it from the case where no meaningful utilization occurs from the evaluation: it is just put on the shelf and forgotten. Note that, as used here, conceptual use obviously occurs in all the program use cases.

Organizational use would occur after an organization has been evaluating its programs for some time. The repeated focus on identifying, measuring, and reporting on program objectives, results, and performance, and the involvement of line managers in the evaluations have resulted in an (increased) acceptance of the usefulness of monitoring and evaluating program performance and of a results-orientation in the management of the organization. This type of organizational impact would imply that the culture of the organization has changed to one more accepting of the need for empirical evidence on the results of programs to manage well. Single- and double-loop learning are becoming part of the organizational culture. For both instrumental and organization use, it is recognized that both the process of evaluation, that is, the carrying out of evaluation activities per se, as well as the findings, conclusions, and recommendations from evaluations can lead to change.

Evaluation utilization is difficult to demonstrate. In trying to attribute to the evaluation the changes that subsequently occur, one is faced with a classic evaluation problem (Smith 1988: 16). Evaluations do not take place in a controlled setting and there are numerous other factors at work which also can legitimately lay claim to "causing" the resulting changes. Program managers, in particular, may wish to claim that they were going to make the changes anyway and that the evaluation did not play a significant role. Indeed, it is usually the case that change will occur in an organization only if there are other factors at work in addition to the evaluation, with the evaluation playing at best a catalyst role. Lindblom and Cohen (1979) have aptly discussed this reality. Most decisions in organizations are based on ordinary knowledge. Knowledge from social science research usually only supplements this.[7]

There are also serious measurement problems. One can undertake a case study to try to determine the impacts of a particular evaluation and the role played by the evaluation. This in itself is a challenging task given the variety of types of utilization that can be sought. But often there is more interest in a global picture of evaluation utilization over time in an organization. Providing detailed case studies on each evaluation usually is not practical. More global assessments of the

impacts of evaluation, however, mean the attribution problem is not addressed.
The result is that it is usually not possible to confirm definitively the "true" impact of evaluation in an organization. Of course, this is the situation normally faced by evaluators. We can at best produce reasonable evidence on utilization and thereby increase the understanding of evaluation practice in an organization. If programs are being improved subsequent to evaluation, many will claim the credit. Determining the value of evaluation utilization will help to clarify those claims.

The Canadian Experience

Program evaluation is carried out in several ways. Much of the utilization literature is based on an external model of evaluation, whereby evaluators are contracted to carry out a particular evaluation.[8] Less analysis has occurred on the internal model of evaluation where an organization has its own evaluators on staff who carry out a program of evaluations in the organization over time. Internal evaluation implies that evaluation activity is part of the management framework in the organization. While a lot of the analysis on utilization may be applicable to both cases, the internal model offers an opportunity to study the extent to which organizations can learn over time from evaluation activities and to explore the ongoing role that evaluation can play in an organization. Sonnichsen in this volume reports a significant growth in internal evaluation activity in the United States and Love (1991) discusses recent experience with the internal model of evaluation.

Evaluation in the government of Canada has been part of the management of departments since 1977. Since then, there has a been a government-wide policy assigning to departments the responsibility to evaluate their own programs over time, to use that information to report on the performance of programs and to make the appropriate changes to improve the performance of programs. The primary client for evaluation is meant to be the head of the organization, the deputy minister. Since 1980, overseeing the policy has been a small group in the Office of the Comptroller General (OCG), part of the central Treasury office, which has provided advice and assistance to departments and has monitored their performance in evaluation.

This institutionalizing of evaluation did not occur overnight. It has evolved considerably over the almost fifteen years the central policy requirement to evaluate has been in place.[9] While some of the evolution represents a maturing and professionalization of evaluation practice in the Canadian federal government, the major changes have been the result of trying to mold evaluation in organizations and across the government to meet the ever-changing demands for information and challenge that evaluation can provide.

By 1991:

- some sixty government institutions, including all major and medium-sized departments had an identified corporate evaluation unit (i.e., not reporting to line management) carrying out evaluations;
- evaluation units varied from one or two people in smaller organizations to an average of ten to fifteen in medium and larger departments and in most cases reported to the head of the organization (deputy minister) or one level down (assistant deputy minister);
- most of the major departments had at least ten years experience with evaluations;
- across government about 80–100 evaluations were being completed annually;
- there were about 350 evaluators across government plus perhaps 100 private consultants contracted by departments working on specific evaluations; and
- as a corporate staff function, program evaluation continued to evolve in response to the changing demands for program performance information.

It is fair to say that almost all Canadian government organizations can identify some evaluation activity. However, the nature, extent and quality of that activity varies considerable across government and, with many organizations, over time as individuals change. While there is a central policy to evaluate, there has always been great flexibility available to departments in how diligent they wish to be regarding the policy.[10] The OCG has promoted the policy based on good management principles—that is, as responding to real demand for information on program results. It has treated the policy less as a requirement and more as good practice, and tried to encourage the use of program evaluation through the utility of evaluation (Office of the Comptroller General 1982). Sanctions for noncompliance are limited, for the most part, to persuasion.

The result is a fairly typical normal curve regarding evaluation practice, with some departments paying lip service to the policy and others carrying out effective evaluations with little thought given to the policy requirement per se. The policy and its monitoring by the OCG have undoubtedly enhanced the establishment of internal evaluation units. But the utilization of evaluation findings cannot be a simple policy requirement. Studying the extent and nature of this utilization across a wide sample of departments provides a number of valuable insights into making internal evaluation work in an organization. Indeed, the wide variation found across the government in the nature and extent of utilization suggests that the existence of a policy itself provides little explanation of utilization.

Given the senior level focus intended, program evaluation in the government of Canada has a broad scope. Evaluation can address:

- *relevance,* the extent to which the program remains consistent with current organizational and government priorities and continues to be seen as a realistic approach to the problem being dealt with;
- *success,* the extent to which the program is meeting its objectives within budget and without undue negative impacts; and
- *cost-effectiveness,* whether the program as delivered is the most cost-effective way to achieve the objectives.

Given this broad scope, a wide variety of utilization can be imagined or expected to take place, from modest operational improvements to a more profound restructuring. Furthermore, the relevance issue is directly aimed at fostering double-loop learning, questioning whether existing program are still needed. Program evaluation in the federal government has been frequently challenged, especially in times of downsizing and restraint, as to the added value it provides. The continued existence of the policy and the evaluation infrastructure in place suggests that evaluation has been found useful and is being used.

Based on data collected by the Office of the Comptroller General, about 210 corporate evaluations completed between 1984 and 1989 from across government departments were examined and followed up to determine the nature and type of utilization that has taken place in the federal government. This represented about one-half of the total number of completed studies during the time period. Departmental evaluation units were asked what happened as a result of the evaluation, but the evidence supplied by the departments was not indepen-

TABLE 1.1
Federal Program Evaluation Summary of Utilization

	1984/87 (%)	89/90 (%)	90/91 (%)	89/90 + 90/91 (%)	Type of Learning
Termination	3	6	4	5	double
Reform	16	13	16	14	double
Modification	45	43	33	38	single
Confirmation	8	8	12	10	single
Understanding	26	25	32	29	double/single
No results	2	5	3	4	none
Totals	100%	100%	100%	100%	

dently confirmed.[11] While the sample was not randomly selected, the general utilization distribution shown was consistent with an earlier analysis conducted of studies completed prior to 1983. More recently, all 178 evaluations completed over two fiscal years (1989/90 and 1990/91) were analyzed on the same basis. The analysis in all cases only looked for program use (not organizational impact).

The resulting data are shown above.

Four types of program instrumental use were used:

- the program was terminated as a result of the evlauation;
- the program underwent major reform as to its design and/or delivery—such as retargetting the program, altering its objectives or decentralizing its delivery—reform that was visible to the clients of the program and changed the nature of the program;
- the program underwent more modest operational modifications—such as streamlining operational procedures, improving information gathering systems, or introducing new procedures—changes often less directly visible to the program clients; and
- the program was basically confirmed as working well.

In addition, conceptual use was identified as evidence that there was an increased understanding in the department of the program and its performance, such as improved reporting on the program, even if no instrumental use was made of the findings. The categories used were "downwardly" mutually exclusive. Thus, "modification" implies that there was no major redesign undertaken but allows for increased understanding to occur. And a study that fell into the "increased understanding" group had no instrumental use. These data confirmed that at least some use was made of the vast majority of evaluations. In addition, evidence (not presented here) suggested that a significant number of the evaluations lead to a reallocation of resources either within the program or within the organization.

While this level of utilization seems to run counter to the image presented in the literature, it is in fact not surprising. Federal departments prepare and submit multiyear plans for evaluation to the Office of the Comptroller General, so that their evaluation intentions are known. Each department has its own evaluation committee made up of the senior executives that meet periodically to consider the findings and recommendations from the evaluations. This combination of known plans and standing evaluation committees makes it difficult for an evaluation to "sit on the shelf" and not be considered by the senior executive of the organization. Thus, as a result of this institutionalizing of evaluation, something organizational tends to happen with almost all evaluations. Debates on evaluation utilization in Canada tend to focus on the distribution of types of utilization that occur rather than on utilization per se.

While the data were not collected with the single- vs. double-loop learning model in mind, the termination and reform categories would closely match double-loop learning, since in both cases the program is significantly restructured. The modification and confirmation categories are clearly single-loop learning cases. Increased understanding might lead eventually to either type of learning. Critics of the federal evaluation process argue that substantially more double-loop learning should occur; that the evaluations too often only focus on single-loop learning (Task Force on Program Review 1986; Sutherland 1990; Savoie 1990: 109–16; Campbell 1991).

Analyzing Evaluation Utilization

In order to understand better the reasons behind the utilization of evaluations in the Canadian federal government and to capture some of the experience gained over the past decade in evaluation, a survey was conducted of the fifteen most experienced heads of evaluation across the federal government.[12]

The survey was aimed at: (a) getting an idea of what "adequate evaluation utilization" should be, and (b) getting a better understanding of what contributes to successful utilization of evaluations in the federal government.

What people expected from evaluation will affect what use is made of evaluation in an organization. However, there are likely many perceptions of what kind and amount of utilization one ought to get from evaluation. The survey addressed the problem by first exploring the perceived expectations for evaluation utilization in organizations, as well as looking at global utilization data across the federal government. This was followed by a series of questions examining the different factors that could affect utilization. Each respondent was interviewed and completed a questionnaire.

Expectations for Evaluation

Respondents were asked to rank in importance a number of possible purposes for evaluation in their organization. This was followed by a discussion of the question. The numerical rankings are summarized in the following table.

Evaluation Purpose	# of the 14 Respondents Ranking the Purpose 1st or 2nd
Corporate challenge/second opinion	3
Aid to strategic planning/policy development	4
Aid to program managers to improve delivery	6
Central Treasury Board requirement	2
Means to account for program performance	4
Means to identify dollar savings	3

Although many viewed evaluation primarily as a tool for assisting program managers to deliver their programs better, there was no general pattern among the respondents. The interesting finding is that, while corporate federal evaluation practice across government falls under the same umbrella Treasury Board policy and in most cases can be said to emanate from that policy, federal evaluation plays different primary roles in different departments.

Through discussion it became clear that evaluation was indeed different in different departments and that the particular characteristic taken by evaluation in a department depended on a number of factors:

- the specific information needs of the organization;
- the management style of the management executive;
- the history of evaluation in the organization;
- the existence and role of other analytical groups;
- the perception of evaluation held by the director of evaluation; and
- the perception of evaluation held by the principle client for evaluation, the deputy head of the organization.

That no government-wide primary purpose for evaluation existed was reinforced by several of the responses that could not be recorded numerically. Several directors had a great difficulty ranking the various purposes since in their view the primary purpose changed from evaluation to evaluation reflecting the specific interests of the department regarding the program at the time of the evaluation. In another case, a primary purpose could be identified, but it had changed over time as the information needs of the department evolved. Furthermore, it was also acknowledged that the nature of evaluation in an organization depends on who controls the issues that are addressed in the evaluations. If, for example, line managers set the evaluation agenda then one should not expect as much significant redesign and elimination of programs to occur.

Thus, successful program evaluation appeared to respond to the perceived information needs of the department. In other words, the supply of evaluation was modified to meet the demand. The broad brush purpose given in Treasury Board policy documents provides the flexibility for different types of evaluation to evolve at different times and different places. Evaluation in an organization can play a variety of roles. Primary purposes ranged from departments that saw evaluation as a control function assessing program performance, to departments that used evaluation more as a form of management consulting to line managers. This variation and adaptability is consistent with Sonnichsen's finding (in this volume) based on analysis of evaluation practice in a number of U.S. government departments and with the conclusion of Kennedy (1983) in an educational evaluation context.

The Nature of Evaluation Utilization

The respondents were asked to comment on the utilization data in Table 1.1. They felt that these utilization data were, on the whole, representative of their department's utilization pattern. This helped confirm the reliability of the data. Utilization from internal evaluation—as opposed to nonutilization—seems the norm and is quite consistent with the antidotal evidence available on evaluation utilization in the Canadian government (Office of the Comptroller General 1991). This is noteworthy since the data on utilization would seem to contradict much evaluation literature regarding the extent of utilization that occurs.

As expected, there was individual variation among the departments, with the "control" departments exhibiting relatively more confirmation use and the "management consulting" departments claiming somewhat more redesign and operational improvement. However, and confirming again that evaluation was different in different departments, there was agreement by all that aiming at a specific target for utilization has little meaning. The type of utilization will vary over time and by department, reflecting the general purpose chosen. Furthermore, it was pointed out that any such target would depend on just what one thinks of the state of government programs: if government programs are thought to be generally in a mess, then one would expect quite different utilization than if programs were thought to be generally alright. Similarly, if resource savings were critical, then one might expect more of that type of utilization.

When asked to describe the major type of impact made on the organization, the majority of respondents did not refer back to the different types of program use (instrumental/conceptual) but in most cases discussed some aspect of organizational impact. That is, the major impact of evaluation seemed to be not so much in the program improvements brought about, particularly the instrumental uses—important though they were—but rather in the longer-term effect on the organization and how it manages generally. Several stressed the importance of conceptual use—the increased understanding gained—and saw the instrumental use as a "bonus." Examples of important organization impacts of evaluation were:

- the long-term impact on the mix of programs and their designs;

Utilizing Evaluation in Organizations 29

- a seed for new ideas, which take some time to be accepted;
- improved understanding of what business the organization is in;
- better objective base of information available on program performance;
- opportunity to reconceptualize programs;
- opportunity to get good feedback from program clientele;
- accelerates program change in the organization; and
- development of a corporate memory and perspective for the organization.

The point was often made that this type of utilization is of course very hard to measure and very hard to attribute to the evaluation function. Everyone wants to claim the benefits from organizational improvement and learning, and the key aim of internal evaluation is to be part of the rganization.

Factors Affecting Utilization

In order to gain some insight on what influences the degree and nature of utilization, respondents were asked to rank and discuss a number of possible factors affecting evaluation utilization. These factors were grouped into three categories: (1) organizational factors; (2) aspects of the process of carrying out evaluations; and (3) the credibility of the evaluations. Respondents—the heads of evaluation in the organization—were asked to assess the relative importance of the factors as influencing utilization and the degree to which they thought they could influence the factor.

The factors suggested were adapted from the general literature such as Cousins and Leithwood (1986), from some similar research conducted by Sonnichsen (1994) at the U.S. federal level, and from Canadian federal experience. Lester and Wilds (1990) provide a synthesis of factors that have been suggested in the literature as influencing research utilization. They use three groupings: contextual (political) factors, technical (methodological) factors of the research and bureaucratic (psychological) factors related to the decision maker(s). There is significant overlap between these and the factors used here, but the Lester and Wilds set focuses more on major sociopolitical factors and neglects many of the process factors considered here. This might reflect the differences between the external vs. internal model of evaluation.

Each of the three groups of factors used in this study was felt by respondents to be important, but the weighting among these general categories revealed no pattern. Quite a few felt that credibility either was a function of the other two or a necessary criteria, although not sufficient for utilization.

Organizational Factors

The factors considered were:

- organizational location of the evaluation group;
- general organizational acceptance of evaluation;
- bureaucratic political factors (office politics);
- the specific individuals involved in an evaluation study; and
- the importance of the program being evaluated.

Respondents were asked to indicate: (a) whether each factor was essential, very important, important, useful, or not relevant; and (b) whether they could control, strongly influence, influence occasionally, or do little regarding each factor.

Each factor, except for the importance of the program, was judged to be important, very important, or essential and all were felt subject to reasonable influence by the director of evaluation. In particular, almost all felt they could at least strongly influence the general organizational acceptance of evaluation in the organization through the marketing and selling of evaluation. The factors considered quite important over which directors felt they had less control were the bureaucratic political factors and the location of the evaluation group, although several felt even these were controllable or could be strongly influenced. Of the other factors mentioned, several alluded to the importance of the leadership shown by the Deputy Minister (DM) or the senior evaluation committee towards evaluation.

Process Factors

The table below identifies the factors considered and summarizes the responses.

The listed factors were all felt to be relevant and affect the attention paid to evaluation and hence to its profile in the organization. It was almost unanimous that involvement of line managers, a surprise free process, and the timeliness of findings were essential or very important

Evaluation Process Factor [selected suggestions for influencing]	Level of Importance	Degree of Control
Involvement of line managers	essential/ very important	very high
A surprise free process [second a program person to the study team]	essential/ very important	very high
The timeliness of the findings [conduct ongoing and extensive scanning within the organization; make preliminary findings available as needed]	essential/ very important	high
Involvement of DM in evaluation process [have available if needed; use sparingly]	very important	high/little
Involvement of program clientele	very important	high
Length of time to conduct studies [break study into smaller parts]	very important/ important	high
Knowledge of evaluation by line managers [educate as needed]	important	high
DM approved Terms of Reference (TOR)	very important/ useful	some
Use of advisory committees [useful for consultation]	important/ not important	very high
Use of consultants	useful/ not important	very high

Ratings shown with a slash (/) indicate the degree of differences among the respondents. Respondents were asked to indicate the importance of the factor as a contribution to utilization of the evaluation's findings and conclusions (essential, very important, important, useful, or not relevant) and the extent they felt that they could positively influence the factor to enhance utilization (can control, strongly influence, influence occasionally, or do little).

factors for utilization. Cousins and Leithwood (1986) reach a similar conclusion. Conversely, use of consultants and knowledge of evaluation by line managers were universally thought not that important. The remaining factors were deemed essential or very important by about half of the respondents.

Most directors felt they had a good degree of control over all of these factors and, not surprisingly, the degree of control was higher than for the organizational factors. Knowledge of evaluation on the part of line managers was described as useful but not that critical because it was felt that managers could be informed about evaluation by the evaluators. In any event, line manager understanding of evaluation was felt capable of being strongly influenced by the evaluation directors. Having terms of reference approved by the head of the organization was judged either quite important or at least useful. However, the type of involvement of the organization head varied in different organizations and the key point mentioned by many respondents was the need for that person to be available if really needed.

Several additional factors not listed in the questionnaire were frequently mentioned as critical. Among them, effective communication inside the organization about the evaluation process and findings was usually thought to be very important, if not essential to utilization. Extensive communication is required for an open evaluation process. Similarly, networking throughout the organization was thought essential in order to be able to properly strategically plan evaluation studies. Several respondents felt that involvement of the second level senior executive managers (assistant deputy ministers) was more important than the involvement of the head of the organization (the deputy minister).

A number of suggestions in addition to normal good practice—careful planning of the evaluation involving the stakeholders, consultation and involvement in the conduct and reporting phases—were offered as factors regarding how best to influence the process. These are listed in the table above. In order to get the timing right, the evaluation unit needs to conduct extensive and ongoing scanning of the decision-making environment, and needs to be willing to present whatever information is on hand if the timing requires it. To control the length of the study better, the study can be broken into smaller parts for which there can be interim findings forthcoming (Winberg 1991). While a few found advisory committees for individual studies not that useful, since grandstanding can take place, most felt that the committees provided a forum for very useful synergy to occur that would be lost in only bilateral meetings. To reduce the threat aspect of evaluation and to enhance the credibility of the evaluation team, it was suggested to borrow persons for the study from the program being evaluated.

Credibility of Evaluation

Respondents were asked to assess the factors and it was assumed that the evaluator could strongly influence or control all of these factors. The table below lists the factors identified and summarizes the responses.

Evaluation Credibility Factors	Level of Importance
Extent to which conclusions followed from the evidence (face validity)	essential/very important
The credibility of the evaluator	very important
The rigor of the methodology used	very important/important
The specific conclusions reached	very important/not relevant
Other factors identified by respondents:	
communication in organizational language	essential/very important
relevance of findings to the organization	essential/very important
involvement of outside experts	sometimes very important

Face validity appeared to be the most important factor affecting credibility in the organization. Rigor was felt important but did not contribute that much to enhancing credibility, although the importance of rigor differed depending on the decision-making context. More important was the credibility of the evaluator who could demonstrate knowledge and understanding of the program and its environment. Other important factors identified were communication of the findings in the language and dominant culture of the organization and the perceived relevance of the issues addressed in the study. In addition, several respondents mentioned the usefulness of involving outside experts in the evaluation process as a way to enhance credibility.

Other Activities Undertaken to Enhance Evaluation

Respondents also were asked what nonevaluation activities they undertake that might influence the use made of evaluation in the organization. Most directors indeed undertook a large number of activities other than evaluation studies that contributed to enhancing the utilization of evaluation in the organization by enhancing its overall credibility. These included:

- other special studies and analysis as requested;
- participating in management planning meetings and conferences;
- speaking to various stakeholder groups about evaluation (networking);
- marketing completed evaluation studies;
- making speeches and preparing publications, attaining outside professional recognition;
- providing advice and assistance to planning and policy groups;
- assistance in other types of program reviews;
- involvement in planning and reporting work; and
- providing advice and opinions on programming matters.

It was felt that a range of activities are required to properly manage the evaluation function. Conner (1988) stresses the importance of the evaluation group being part of the regular order of business in an organization.

Obstacles to and Opportunities for Utilization

As might be expected, a range of obstacles was mentioned, (although resources for evaluation were never mentioned!). Among the obstacles discussed:

- a shortage of resources available to implement the program changes;
- information overload for senior managers (more performance information available than can be assimilated and used);
- the general difficulty to change the status quo in an organization;
- the difficulty of getting the timing of the findings right due to unanticipated agenda setting by the minister, the length of time required to

complete studies, and the difficulty in making legislative changes; and
- too much control of the evaluation process by program managers who do not want change to occur.

When asked about opportunities for enhancing evaluation utilization, no new insights emerged, rather a recapitulation of some of the points made earlier. One needs to work to change attitudes toward evaluation in the organization. Better strategic planning of the evaluations can increase the likelihood they will fit better into the organization's decision-making agenda. A director of evaluation who is competent in marketing evaluation can improve utilization.

Survey Conclusions

Several general conclusions of the survey stand out. As we have seen, successful internal evaluation adapts to the organizational environment so as to be responsive to the current information needs of the organization. However, successful internal evaluation requires considerable marketing of evaluation within the organization since evaluation is not a natural organizational activity (Wildavsky 1985). Finally, internal evaluation can play a significant role in influencing the demand in an organization for evaluation information.

This last conclusion differs somewhat from the findings of Lester and Wilds (1990: 317) who conclude that "most of the variables affecting knowledge utilization are outside the control of the analysts." They do speculate, however, that future research might discover "that these [contextual and bureaucratic] factors can be manipulated by the analysts" in which case more could be done to enhance utilization. Our study suggests this is so.

Evaluation Demand and Supply

In discussing organizational learning from evaluation, a useful analogy can be borrowed from economics. There, a basic tenet is that markets will clear—and hence be efficient and effective—when the supply of goods or services meets the demand for it. Much economic behavior is analyzed and explained using this simple model. We would argue that the utilization of evaluation can be profitably discussed and explained using this supply-demand model: evaluations will be used when the supply of evaluation information meets the demand for such information. More specifically, the findings and conclusions from evaluations will be used to improve the performance of a program only when there is a specific demand for information about the performance of the program by those who can actually affect the program and that demand is met by evaluations that supply the information in a credible and timely manner.

While conceptually simple, as in economics, this supply-demand model contains quite a few complex and sophisticated concepts about evaluation and organizations that might make use of it. The "market" envisaged here is the political/bureaucratic decision-making regime in an organization and the "price" is the value placed by the organization on the evaluation information that is produced. The organization will only consider information, or place a "value" on it, if it is seen as useful and timely. When evaluation information produced has a value—or perhaps expected value—equal to the "need" for information, then utilization of evaluation will take place. Utilization will take place until the marginal cost of the information exceeds the marginal value for further information.

One could explain the market for evaluation in a number of ways. Considerable evaluation practice, and most evaluation research, is based on a supply-push assumption, whereby the supply of good evaluations is assumed to create a demand for the information, resulting in utilization. And a program evaluation that produces forceful and credible findings might by itself generate sufficient attention that program change occurs. However, there is a lot of evidence that in most organizations this is the exception rather than the rule, even in organizations that traditionally see information and evidence as a legitimate part of decision making. It is asking too much in most cases for organizational decision making to conform to the production of evaluation information.

Alternatively, a demand-pull framework would claim that if the demand for evaluative information in an organization is made clear, then evaluations will be produced to fill the gap. And perhaps this is the conceptual framework behind the external evaluation model discussed at the beginning of the chapter. An organization decides it needs certain evaluative information and proceeds to hire an outside evaluator to produce it.

Effective internal evaluation is perhaps based on a model that tries to balance supply and demand, whereby the organization's evaluators both attempt to supply information that meets demand but also try to influence the demand for evaluative information. We have seen that the Canadian federal experience is consistent with this view. Most of the internal evaluators interviewed felt they could and should influence the demand for evaluation, as well as try to match the supply in order to reach the right balance. And balance is the operative word.

The Supply of Evaluations

The classic imbalance that plagues much evaluation is the supply of evaluations where or when there is no corresponding demand for the program performance information. Evaluations are done and not used. We know that with resources, evaluation studies can be produced, with more or less elegance.

The evaluation literature is full of advice to evaluators as to how to improve their products: write clearly, be timely, produce defensible findings, and so forth.[13] And much of it is good but incomplete advice. Its volume is undoubtedly due to the fact that it is addressing that part of the utilization problem over which evaluators feel they have considerable control. Evaluators can and should endeavor to improve the quality of evaluations as much as possible. But it will often be to no avail, if equal attention is not directed to the demand side of the equation.

The Demand for Evaluation Information

The demand side has been much less well discussed. This is understandable since it deals with matters beyond traditional evaluation expertise and in areas that seemingly are not under the control of the evaluator.[14] As we have seen, in most cases, many of the factors affecting demand are or can be under the influence of the evaluator. And the design of an evaluation fails if it does not take into account the organizational reality of the demand—or lack of it—for information on the program.

Furthermore, demand for evaluative information may not be easily identified. A program manager or senior executive may be able to say what kind of information he or she wants and when. But this is only the immediate demand. An internal evaluator can also try and antici-

38   Can Governments Learn?

pate future demand for performance information about the program, based on experience in the organization and the policy area, and knowledge about performance information needed in other programming areas.

The Balancing Act

Elsewhere in this book, the concepts of organizational learning are discussed. As outlined earlier, organizations undertake single-loop learning when they are able to modify their operations in light of evidence that their program goals are not being met. They undertake double-loop learning when they are able to reorient their aims and objectives—and then their operations—as a result of evidence they acquire on the efficacy of their current operations.

Organizations that do learn have clearly been able to match their demand for performance information with its supply. They are able to balance the two and achieve a particular level and nature of organizational learning. And, of course, the balance achieved can result either in significant learning and changes (double-loop learning) or in more modest learning and changes (single-loop learning).

The data in table 1.1 provides some evidence on the extent of each type of organizational learning in the government of Canada. As indicated earlier, the data suggest that perhaps 20 percent of the evaluations lead to double-loop learning (program termination and major program reform), and at least 45 percent to single-loop learning (program modification).[15] That double-loop learning has occurred should not be surprising since evaluations that do address the issues of relevance or the cost-effectiveness of a program are challenging the basic raison d'être of the program. Those that address the success of programs might be expected to lead most often to single-loop learning.

The extent to which a particular organization is able to learn obviously depends on a number of factors: the history of change in the organization, the management style, the aims of the organization, and so forth. And its willingness to learn will strongly influence its demand for information on its performance. So the extent to which evaluators can influence the demand for performance information is clearly limited and will vary from organization to organization and over time.

If an organization is not interested in change and resists evidence that suggests change, it is unlikely that evaluation will be a significant part of the organization; it is then a moot point whether or not evaluation would be utilized since little or no evaluation is occurring. On the other hand, organizations that do value review and evidence on their performance—that undertake single- or double-loop learning—will at least consider evaluation as a potentially useful management tool for change. In these cases, the supply-demand model suggests that utilization can be enhanced if the evaluator endeavors to understand and influence this demand for information, as well as design the evaluations to best match the demand in terms of the issues addressed, timeliness, and degree of rigor.

Furthermore, if the demand for information is taken more broadly than the apparent immediate demand, balancing supply and demand also allows for the experienced internal evaluator to supply some evaluation information that he or she anticipates will be called for in the future. Such a strategy involves some risk, of course, but if the evaluator has become the main corporate memory on program performance and is successful a few times in anticipating demand, this temporary oversupply of information will not cause a problem.

From the survey findings, we have seen that influencing the demand for evaluation is possible and could include a range of activities:

- being knowledgeable about and helping to articulate current and planned performance-related issues in the organization in terms of the dominant organization culture;
- attempting to alter the timing of a performance-related decision by being able to promise practical performance information at a specific time, and delivering on time;
- marketing program evaluation by demonstrating the kind of information that it can and has produced on organizational performance;
- establishing a corporate memory on the past performance of the organization's programs;
- making sure at least some information on performance is available when the demand arises; and
- marketing the evaluation findings from specific studies to show that it does indeed meet reasonably well the information needed by the organization to make decisions on future programming.

Sonnichsen's (1988) advocacy evaluation model is in part trying to influence the kind of information "demanded" by the organization.

Conclusions

Management styles and systems change over time both within organizations and across government. If evaluation is to remain useful and be used, it must adapt to the existing organizational situation. Neither organizations nor programs exist in order to be evaluated. However, an evaluation function in an organization over time can exert a real influence on factors that affect the extent to which utilization of evaluation occurs. Most importantly, evaluation needs to be strategically planned and then extensively marketed in an organization. A credible evaluation function that is seen as a useful and important part of the management of an organization can influence the articulation and the demand for performance information. In this way, evaluators can go some way to balancing their supply of relevant information with the organization demand.

Notes

1. Much of the interesting literature on utilization addresses the larger question of the utilization of research by public policy decision makers. Lester and Wilds (1990) provide a synthesis and critique of this literature. A recent review of the specific evaluation literature on utilization can be found in McLaughlin et al. (1988).
2. See Patton (1988), Weiss (1988), and Alkin (1990).
3. The term *program* as used in this chapter, should be interpreted broadly, as covering a variety of possible types of government instruments, such as expenditure activities, regulations, and tax expenditures as well as different possible levels of programming, from straightforward operations to major programs to policies (collections of programs with a common aim).
4. Cordray and Lipsey (1986) and Schwandt (1990) discuss and explore this distinction using the terms *program evaluation* vs. *program research.*
5. Single- and double-loop learning are introduced in the introduction, and discussed later in this chapter.
6. The definitions used here are not exactly the same as those of Rich (1977) who introduced these terms. A more demanding definition of instrumental use is used here in relation to internal evaluation, which is akin to the impact-type of utilization discussed by Leviton and Hughes (1981). Leviton distinguishes utilization from impact and utility, with utilization implying merely that findings were considered.
7. See also the discussion by Carol Weiss in Alkin (1990: 22, 43).
8. *External evaluation,* as the term is used here, is program evaluation rather than evaluation research, since the organization is deciding on the evaluation agenda. If

it abrogates this responsibility then it is likely to get a piece of evaluation research done, reducing the chances of program use following.
9. Segsworth (1990) and McQueen (1992) provide descriptions and analysis of the Canadian federal government's experience with evaluation. An assessment of progress was made by the Auditor General of Canada in 1983.
10. This policy was recently revised and approved by the Treasury Board of Canada (1992).
11. A recent Office of Comptroller General (OCG) publication (1991) documents the use made of a selection of evaluation studies.
12. The individuals interviewed represented sixteen departments since several had been director of evaluation in more than one organization. Departments represented included Agriculture, Transport, Customs and Excise, Indian and Northern Affairs, Consumer and Corporate Affairs, Employment and Immigration, Fisheries and Oceans, Justice, Public Service Commission, Mortgage and Housing, International Development, Communications, Energy, Mines and Resources, Veterans Affairs and the National Research Council.
13. Smith (1988) provides an overview of recent advice to improve utilization. Mayne and Mayne (1985) discuss adapting program evaluation to best fit the policy formulation process.
14. Mowbray (1988) discusses the unpreparedness of evaluators to market their work and the need for evaluators to do much more than "evaluate."
15. We would argue that cases where an evaluation confirms a program as working well are cases of single-loop learning, and if the program rationale has been seriously challenged and found solid, than double-loop learning is being practiced.

References

Alkin, M. C. 1990. *Debates on Evaluation*. Newbury Park, CA: Sage.
Auditor General of Canada. 1983. *Annual Report*. Chapter 3. Ottawa.
Bulmer, M. 1982. *The Uses of Social Research: Social Investigation in Public Policy-Making*. Boston: Allen & Unwin.
Campbell, D. R. 1991. "Program Management and Program Evaluation." Prepared for the Centre for Management Development. Ottawa.
Conner, R. F. 1988. "Structuring Knowledge Production Activities to Facilitate Knowledge Utilization: Thoughts on Important Utilization Issues." *Studies in Educational Evaluation* 14: 273–83.
Cordray, D. S., and M. W. Lipsey. 1986. "Program Evaluation and Program Research." In *Evaluation Studies Review Annual,*. no. 11 ed. C. A. Lipsey. Newbury Park, CA: Sage.
Cousins, J. B., and K. A. Leithwood. 1986. "Current Empirical Research on Evaluation Utilization." *Review of Educational Research* 56, no. 3: 331–64.

Kennedy, M. M. 1983. "The Role of the In-House Evaluator." *Evaluation Review* 7, no. 4 (August): 519–41.

Lester, J. P., and L. J. Wilds. 1990. "The Utilization of Public Policy Analysis: A Conceptual Framework." *Evaluation and Program Planning* 13: 313–19.

Leviton, L. C., and E. F. X. Hughes. 1981. "Research on the Utilization of Evaluation: A Review and Synthesis." *Evaluation Review* 5, no. 4: 525–48.

Lindblom, L. C., and Cohen, D. K. 1979. *Usable Knowledge.* New Haven, CT: Yale University Press.

Love, A. J. 1991. *Internal Evaluation.* San Francisco: Sage.

McLaughlin, J. A., L. J. Weber, R. W. Covert, and R. B. Ingle. (Ed.). 1988. *Evaluation Utilization: New Directions for Program Evaluation,* no. 39. San Francisco: Jossey-Bass.

Mayne, J., and R. S. Mayne. 1985. "Will Program Evaluation be Used in Policy Formulation?" In *The Politics of Canadian Public Policy,* ed. M. M. Atkinson and M. A. Chandler 267–83. Toronto: University of Toronto Press.

McQueen, C. 1992. "Organizing for Program Evaluation in the Canadian Federal Government, In *Action-Oriented Evaluation in Organizations: Canadian Practices,* ed. J. Hudson, J. Mayne, and R. Thomlison. Toronto: Wall & Emerson.

Mowbray, C. T. 1988. "Getting the System to Respond to Evaluation Findings." In *Evaluation Utilization,* ed. J. A. McLaughlin, L. J. Weber, R. W. Covert, and R. B. Ingle. San Francisco: Jossey-Bass.

Office of the Comptroller General. 1982. *Guide on the Program Evaluation Policy.* Ottawa: Treasury Board.

———. 1991. *Evaluation Compendium: Evaluation Utilization in the Federal Government.* Ottawa: Treasury Board.

Patton, M. Q. 1988. "The Evaluator's Responsibility for Utilization." *Evaluation Practice* 11: 141–48.

Rich, R. F. 1977. "Uses of Social Science Information by Federal Bureaucrats: Knowledge for Actions versus Knowledge for Understanding." In *Using Social Science Research in Public Policy,* ed. C. H. Weiss. Lexington, MA: Lexington Books.

Rist, R. C., ed. 1990. *Program Evaluation and the Management of Government.* New Brunswick, NJ: Transaction Publishers.

Savoie, D. 1990. *The Politics of Public Spending in Canada.* Toronto: Toronto University Press.

Schwandt, T. A. 1990. "Defining 'Quality' in Evaluation." *Evaluation and Program Planning* 13: 177–88.

Segsworth, R. 1990. "Policy and Program Evaluation in the Government of Canada." In *Program Evaluation.* See Rist 1990.

Smith, M. F. 1988. "Evaluation Utilization Revisited." In *Evaluation Utilization: New Directions in Program Evaluation,* no. 39, ed. J.A. McLaughlin, L. J.

Weber, R. Covert, and R. B. Ingle, 7–19. San Francisco: Jossey-Bass.
Sonnichsen, R. C. 1988. "Advocacy Evaluation: A Model for Internal Evaluation Offices." *Evaluation and Program Planning* 11: 141–48.
———. 1994. "Effective Internal Evaluation: An Approach to Organizational Learning." In *Can Governments Learn?: Comparative Perspectives on Evaluation and Organizational Learning,* ed. F. L. Leeuw, R. C. Rist, and R. Sonnichsen. New Brunswick, NJ: Transaction Publishers.
Sutherland, S. L. 1990. "The Evolution of Ideas in Canada: Does Parliament Benefit from Estimates Reform?" *Canadian Public Administration* 33, no. 2: 133–46.
Task Force on Program Review. 1986. *An Introduction to the Process of Program Review*. Ottawa: Supply and Services Canada.
Treasury Board of Canada. 1992. *Program Evaluation Policy*. Treasury Board Manual, Evaluation and Audit Branch. Ottawa: Supply and Services.
Trevor-Roper, H., and G. Urban. 1989. "Aftermaths of Empire: The Lessons of Upheavals and Destabilization." *Encounter* (December): 3–16.
Weiss, C. H. 1977. "Research for Policy's Sake: The Enlightenment Function of Social Research." *Policy Analysis* 3, no. 4, 531–45.
———. 1988. "Evaluation for Decisions: Is Anybody There? Does Anybody Care?" *Evaluation Practice* 9 (February): 5–19.
Wildavsky, A. 1985. "The Self-Evaluating Organization." In *Program Evaluation: Patterns and Directions,* ed. E. Chelimsky, 246–65. Washington, DC: American Society for Public Administration.
Winberg, A. 1991. "Maximizing the Contribution of Internal Evaluation Units." *Evaluation and Program Planning* 14: 167–72.

2

Learning from Evaluations: The Swedish Experience

Jan-Eric Furubo

Evaluation activities in Sweden have been molded in a political setting steeped in optimistic views with respect to the capacity of the state and public bodies to tackle various problems. This optimism has been coupled with a very strong belief in the possibility of making rational decisions on the basis of reports and analyses.

In this chapter we shall examine the extent to which the results obtained from evaluations are introduced into administrative and political decision-making processes, and the organizational arrangements by which this is done. We shall also examine the extent to which evaluations are actually made use of and consider whether those evaluations that are used provide examples—using terms discussed in the introductory chapter—of single- or double-loop learning.

Before doing this, it may prove useful to sketch briefly the structure of public administration in Sweden. Public administration at the national level in Sweden is distinct from that in many other countries. In Sweden a very clear distinction is made between ministries and agencies, reflecting the idea of the separability of politics from administration. In international terms, Swedish ministries are very small, and as a rule they rarely employ more than 200 people. The aggregate activities of the ministries do not therefore occupy more than about 2,000 individuals. To a great extent, therefore, the tasks of the ministries may be characterized by their emphasis on policy formulation. Proposals to be laid before Parliament are elaborated within the ministries. This means that the ministries have the task of ordering information from agency sources to buttress the decisions of the government and Parliament. But in a strictly formal perspective, even this kind of order may only be issued by the Cabinet as a collective body.

Implementing the decisions of Parliament or the government is, on the other hand, a task falling to the various agencies. There is a large number of agencies and their size varies quite considerably. Some agencies number their employees in the thousands. In a second group of seventy to eighty agencies, the number of people employed may be anything from 100 to several hundred. Finally, there are more than 1,000 agencies with only a few employees, in certain cases no more than a handful. Many agencies are also subdivided into regional and local departments.

In their day-to-day work, the agencies are relatively autonomous vis-à-vis the ministries. In concrete terms this means that the government is in principle unable to intervene in the processing of individual cases. This relative autonomy is illustrated by the fact that agency executives and heads (directors-general and similar officials) are normally appointed for a period of six years, their mandate being unaffected even if elections go against the government that appointed them. Experience has also shown that in many cases new governments have retained previously appointed agency heads even when they have had the chance of swapping them for others.

If we view these relationships in a formal perspective, decisions with respect to public administration activities are taken at two different levels, namely by the agencies or by the government and Parliament. At the level of government and Parliament it may be appropriate to distinguish between two types of decision-making processes. One is the budget process through which resources are allocated to agencies. The other decision-making process at this level may then be regarded as comprising the challenges faced in adopting fundamental positions with respect to the existence, dimensions, and orientation of various policy activities in which central government may become involved. While the budget process is a regular and recurrent process, the more fundamental policy-making processes have a more ad hoc character, and their occurrence depends very much on the place they occupy on the political agenda. Policy questions often involve areas relating to several different agencies.

By using this distinction between the budget process and more fundamental reassessments, we are in essence employing the same approach as those who have a marginalist view of the budget process, such as Wildavsky (1986), for instance. We consider this view to have empirical validity on the basis of our observations of Swedish experience. In the analysis carried out in 1985 that preceded the advent of the new budget process in Sweden, it was ascertained that in the normal run of things extremely few thorough reassessments of activities have occurred in conjunction with regular budget work (SOU 1985). The analysis indicates two explanations for this. The first is the pressure to meet deadlines within the ministries in connection with the budget work. The second is that the agencies lack the capacity or motivation to propose comprehensive and long-term changes in their own activities within the framework of the budget process.

The second explanation may be enlarged upon. It is possible to regard the budget process as something strongly bound to the existing structure within which central government activities are pursued. Basically, the materials for the budget process are gathered by the agencies themselves. To a great degree the assessment concerns the question of to what extent resources should be added to the *existing structure* and the activities pursued within it.

It would seem natural to argue that fundamental reassessments more or less by definition involve the possibility of questioning the existing structure. The problems are viewed from a different perspective. If the goals are challenged, it is self-evident that a structure erected around certain given means will also be subject to reassessment. This very much applies even if the goals persist while the means are called into question.

In discussing ways in which decision makers learn from evaluations, it would therefore seem to be worth distinguishing between different decision-making processes. In the present context we shall therefore distinguish between:

- thorough going, fundamental policy decisions made by the government and Parliament with regard to whether the state should influence developments in a sphere of activities (and the goals to be set in that case), the selection of policy instruments, for example;

- budget decisions made by the government and Parliament, by which resources are allocated to various activities and agencies; and
- decisions within the agencies.

These three decision-making processes are all supplied with evaluations from various sources.

Evaluations in Various Decision-Making Processes

Table 2.1 provides an overview of the sources of evaluation most closely connected with the various decision-making processes.

TABLE 2.1
Main Sources of Evaluation and Decision-Making Process

Evaluation Sources Decision-Making Process	Commissions	Research Bodies within a Sector	Agencies with Evaluations as a Main Task	Agencies in General
Fundamental policy decisions	X	X	X	
Budget process			X	X
Agency decision-making				X

Evaluation In Relation to Fundamental Policy Decisions

With respect to fundamental policy decisions, there are several sources able to contribute evaluations. Traditionally, policy decisions with more fundamental implications have often been prepared by specially appointed ad hoc policy commissions. A commission system resembling that existing today had already begun to take form in the seventeenth century (Johansson 1992: 3)

Today, the Swedish commission system may be said to be unusually comprehensive in scope. There are few countries that employ specially appointed commissions to the same extent in the preparation of proposed reforms. Finland, which in part shares the same administrative tradition as Sweden, is perhaps the nearest equivalent. The Swedish commission system has played a central role in the preparation of political decisions during the whole of this century (Meijer, 1956: 8; and DSSB 1984: 1). It celebrated its greatest triumphs, however, in the 1960s and 1970s with over 300 commissions working annually. In recent years, almost 200 different commissions have been at work annually (Petersson 1988: 8).

If we consider developments over a comparatively long period of time, we may ascertain that practically every question of any significance has been prepared in a commission. The commissions involved often contain representatives of the political parties and major interest groups. But another feature of the commission system in Sweden that appears significant in this context is the great importance attached to the collection of various kinds of factual material. The commission system can in this way also be regarded as a major channel for introducing knowledge of the current state of research in various fields of activity into the political decision-making process.[1]

Within the framework of the system of public official inquiries in Sweden we find in various research reports and statements of expert opinion not a few examples of what we have more recently designated as evaluations, even when we go back to the 1950s and the 1960s, or indeed even earlier. They are often to be found under such headings as "previous experience," "the current situation," and so forth. There have been no systematic studies made of these early appearances of evaluation in the Swedish commission system.

While preparing this chapter, however, I went through the sixty-five reports that were published by various commissions in 1945. Almost all of them published various kinds of statistical material related to the question under discussion. As a rule they also contained statistics regarding state activities in the field being studied. If the question involved state grants for school buildings, for instance, the reader would be presented with a considerable amount of information about both school buildings and the various grants paid to the municipalities, and perhaps about their distribution to different kinds of local authorities.

A number of these reports also presented empirical material with a view to eliciting whether or not there existed any causal relation between previously decided central government measures and their effects. It was possible to observe a number of unambiguous examples of evaluations—as defined above—in the 1945 material. Among these were:

- A study was undertaken by the special commission set up by the gov-

ernment in 1942 to review the effectiveness of postinstitutional care for delinquent young people who had been in the care of special juvenile institutions. Changes in the organization of corrective homes decided by Parliament in 1936 and 1937 were studied with particular reference to the effect they had had on the duration of the care given, the education of the youngsters concerned, and their subsequent working careers.
- The population inquiry commissioned in 1941 concluded that it was important to create the preconditions for an "unprejudiced discussion of the economic effects of social policy on the life of society." This resulted in the publication in 1945 of a study that among other things dealt with the direct significance of social policy for the distribution of income.
- The education inquiry of 1940 discussed experience accumulated in relation to the then existing centrally regulated marking system. One of the components of the inquiry was a study of the value of academic grades as a forecasting instrument, in which students who had matriculated at three grammar schools between 1872 and 1892 were ranked with respect to their examination grades and subsequent professional achievement using a distribution whose major categories were "outstanding" and "notoriously unsuccessful."

There also existed an awareness of what we may call the fundamental problems of evaluation long before evaluations began to be referred to as such in Sweden, as is shown by the following quotation from an official inquiry in 1934 concerning the possibility of seeing the effects of certain measures of financial regulation. The author declares that an inquiry of this kind into the effects of the regulation:

> must relate the difference between the economic events which would be triggered by the employment of a different regulation. This other regulation (the norm of comparison) must therefore also be specified. In any other sense than as a difference between two sets of events initiated by alternative measures of financial regulation, all talk of effects will be devoid of definite content. (Myrdal 1934: 8)

A scientific approach to the assessment of the effects of various measures of public intervention can therefore by no means be considered a radically new departure. On the other hand, it was not until the early years of the 1960s that evaluation came to be viewed as an activity that might continuously provide politicians and other decision makers with the briefing materials required for reassessments planned for in advance. An example may be given to illustrate this. After the introduction of the compulsory nine-year comprehensive school system in 1962, the Swedish Board of Education was given the responsibility of continuously monitoring the development of the system and thereby evaluating it. The intention was that the evaluations would provide the factual basis for successive revisions of the school system's general curricula (Wikberg and Lundgren 1980: 17).

But the school system was not the only sector where it was intended to bring evaluation activities into the decision-making process in a more continuous fashion. As early as the 1960s, many discussions were conducted concerning the effects of various instruments of social and consumer policy with a view to enabling the most disadvantaged groups to obtain real benefits from them. Thus, an interest in questions of evaluation was developing in several different policy areas, as part of what we may call an intrasectoral development process. This led to the creation of research bodies in a number of sectors, such as for example construction, crime prevention, and energy, with evaluation as one of their principal tasks. Parallel to ideas of evaluation gaining a foothold within several specific policy areas in this way, a more general or suprasectoral grasp of the questions involved was maturing.

In certain areas individual agencies have also been allotted a similar role as central evaluation bodies independent of their more operative tasks in the implementation of policy in the sector in question. In these cases therefore it is a question of agencies that have the task of examining the developments in a certain area of society in general terms and not in relation to their own activities. It may be stated that the task of evaluation in these cases is a special one lying outside the range of the other activities pursued by the agency.

Evaluations in the Budget Process

Beginning in the late 1960s, this interest in the ways in which evaluations might continuously provide decision makers with material has given rise to an endeavor to introduce various kinds of evaluation into the budget process. Having been strictly a fiscal process, the budget process was to become a process in which the responsibilities of the various agencies would be gauged on the basis of experience gained by balancing costs against results. In this sense the budget process would become a learning process.

The first attempt at establishing a budgetary philosophy of this kind occurred when a proposal for the introduction of program budgeting was submitted in 1967. To summarize the experience of this early effort, we may note with the benefit of hindsight that the fundamentally rationalistic model represented by program budgeting in the textbook version propounded in the 1967 report was not in fact realized in more than a very few cases Riksrevisionsverket (RRV 1975).

It is, however, possible to point out a number of consequences of the contributions made in the late 1960s:

- first, cost awareness, alternative projections, and long-term planning won a footing in the budget process;
- a second consequence was the advent of the Swedish performance audit, which has a great many of the characteristics of program evaluation; and
- finally, a consequence of no small significance was a growth of interest in the budget process as a decision-making process. For this reason the question of the budget process is raised in several reports on the Swedish administrative system during the 1970s and 1980s.

And at the end of the 1980s it was once more time to try to transform the budget process into a process in which the adjustment of various aspects of policy would also be regarded as a self-evident feature. The central component in this new budget system is an annual report in which the agencies provide a fairly detailed account of various performance measurements. Alongside this report the agencies are to submit an in-depth budget request, including not only a properly devised account of results achieved over the immediately preceding years but also a detailed plan of proposed results for the following years. Normally this in-depth budget request is to be submitted every third year, but in the case of small agencies less frequent submissions are considered sufficient, with a maximum interval between reports of six years.[2]

An important part of the preparations for these more detailed studies involves agencies being presented with directives from their respective ministries in the year before they are to draw up their in-depth budget requests. These directives include requests for information on any aspects of the agency's activities the ministries may wish to know about. At the same time the ministries are also able to make use of other independent evaluation bodies, such as the National Audit Bureau's administrative audit, the Agency for Administrative Development, the previously mentioned sectoral bodies, and others, to help in assessing agency activities.

The fact that various activities taking place in the agencies will be subject to more probing examination means that the new budget process will have consequences for the relationship between the budget process and the other decision-making processes discussed above. Now that ministries are able to obtain briefing materials of higher quality and ministerial officials are able to devote more time to each individual agency and each individual activity, it should be possible to deal with some of the matters previously referred to special inquiries within the budget process itself.

This means that the role of the ministries will change. Their part in the budget process will become more analytically oriented and less involved with budgetary technicalities. The ministries will have to be able to make clear to the agencies, in a way they have not been obliged to previously, just what information they require from them—and from others. The success or otherwise of the new budget process will therefore depend on the extent to which ministries actually make use of the material they receive. In other words: is the budget process capable of becoming a continuous learning process?

Evaluation in Relation to Agency Decision Making

Another major area for making use of evaluations is to be found in the agencies themselves. The new triennial budget process involves decentralization to the agencies. To a greater extent, decisions on technical and instrumental matters related to achieving the goals set for agencies by central government are to be made within the agencies themselves. Evaluations that may be utilized in the agencies' own decision making may be said to be based on an internal perspective, in other words, the evaluations are directed inward toward the agencies as production systems and toward the relation between resources and output. It is a matter of observing the actual process of production, the development of production, and so forth. The ultimate purpose of these evaluations is to assess whether the agencies are "doing correctly what has to be done."

In 1992 the National Audit Bureau published a study of state evaluation activities. On the basis of a survey of a selection of agencies carried out in 1989, the study concluded that 65 percent of the agencies had had some involvement with evaluations using an internal perspective (RRV 1991).

The study was based on different kinds of source materials. In the first place, four case studies were carried out in which the types of evaluations performed in relation to various social commitments were scrutinized. Second, a survey of agencies was undertaken in the autumn of 1988 and the spring of 1989. The main focus of the survey was to study how the agencies had organized their evaluations. The survey contained questions addressing such issues as the way in which the agencies had involved themselves in the evaluations, the matters they had taken care of themselves and those they had left to others, and the use they had made of evaluations. The survey was sent to thirty-two agencies, including eight that had participated in the trials of the new budget process. Answers were received from twenty-six agencies. The first part contained a number of more general questions concerning the evaluations undertaken in the agency's sphere of activities. The second part of the survey was a questionnaire to be filled in for each separate evaluation that had been carried out in the previous three years, although the number of analyses about which we requested this more detailed information was limited to ten per agency. In this way we acquired more detailed information on 100 separate results analyses in all.[3]

With respect to most of the evaluations employing an internal perspective, the agencies themselves took the initiative. If the initiative was taken by the agencies themselves, it usually came from the relevant ministry. It was usually the case that the agencies themselves carried out the evaluations. If another evaluator was chosen, it was usually a firm of consultants or the Agency for Administrative Development.

But even where it was a question of evaluations intended to aid intra-agency decision making, interest was focused on the external perspective. It is, for instance, self-evident that an agency attempting to influence the way companies use energy has an interest in knowing how companies receive and process information and the measures this may lead to.

In these cases, too, the agencies appeared as the most significant initiators. It was, however, more common for the agencies to commission outside bodies or individuals such as consultancies or researchers to carry out such evaluations. This occurred in roughly half of the cases. It was difficult to discern any pattern with respect to the type of evaluations entrusted to outsiders. In one case, which involved an analysis of violence and threats against inmates of correctional institutions, the fact that the responsible agency itself did not carry out the evaluation was motivated by a reference to the problem in question being of a sensitive nature. In a number of cases, reference was made to the lack of relevant competence or institutional arrangements within the agency for handling evaluation.

An interesting observation in relation to the discussion concerning evaluations with an internal or an external perspective respectively, is that there would not appear to be any relationship between these two categories. At agency level it would seem to be a matter of two different phenomena that have developed separately and independently of each other. This has to do with different traditions and commitments in various parts of an agency. The internal perspective seems most frequently used for an agency's financial and administrative functions, whereas the external perspective was most often used where the questions addressed the agency's operational functions.

Do Decision Makers Learn from Evaluations?

We have described above what would appear to be a well-developed system for introducing the results of evaluations into various political and administrative decision-making processes. But our fundamental question in the present context also concerns the extent to which decision makers in fact learn from evaluations. In other words, have evaluations led to visible changes of position in various policy areas?

To begin with, let us make two fundamental observations. First, we are able to ascertain that the greater part of the evaluations performed are quite clearly oriented toward one of the three decision-making processes discussed above. In the 1988-89 survey of agencies noted earlier concerning evaluations in their own sphere of activities, we obtained more detailed information on 100 separate evaluations. In almost all of these cases it was possible to link the evaluations with one of the three decision-making processes.

In a number of individual cases, the intended use was such that the utility of the evaluation did not depend on whether or not it was to be used in various administrative or political decision-making processes. For example, in one or two cases, the stated purpose was to stimulate public debate. In a number of other cases, the evaluations were undertaken with the aim of disseminating various techniques and methods of work. The National Board for Consumer Policies referred to having carried out evaluations of different kinds of counseling activities in order to spread certain methods of counseling to other local authorities. This was a question of using the evaluations as an instrument of information, presenting a "good example" in order to influence people beyond the circle of state decision makers in central government.

But these are exceptions. More than 90 percent of the evaluations covered by the 1988-89 survey were intended for use as briefing materials for political and administrative decisions in central government. When the agencies were asked about the actual use they made of the evaluations ("How have the studies actually been used?"), the answers were formulated in the same terms as the intended use. No comprehensive studies with an exclusive focus on the issue of use have been undertaken in Sweden, but some studies have touched upon the question and provide some basis for introducing a discussion of a more hypothetical character.

First, we shall make an important observation on the character of the 100 evaluations included in the study mentioned above, on the basis of which we may judge what type of learning, if any, may have occurred as a result of the evaluation. A very small proportion of the 100 evaluations examined contain any discussion at all of the underlying assumptions of the various activities involved. The National Audit Bureau's study in 1992 considers it doubtful whether any of the individual evaluations studied in greater detail were concerned with the theoretical validity of various central government endeavors. The study summarized its findings this way:

> Only exceptionally—in let us say four or five cases—is there reason to believe that the analyses have been intended to serve as the basis for fundamental reassessments of various activities. To a great extent therefore the evaluations undertaken have been envisaged as aids to adopting a position within the framework of the fundamental tasks devolving on the various agencies. (National Audit Bureau 1992)

These observations in themselves restrict as it were the potential area for the occurrence of double-loop learning in the sense of evaluations providing more knowledge about the fundamental assumptions underlying various activities. A similar observation is made in a recent dissertation published in the spring of 1992 on the Swedish commission system during the period 1955-89 (Johansson 1992). In this context Johansson reaches the conclusion that the greater part of the knowledge accumulated within the commission system is not regarded as relating to fundamental premises for various central government endeavors, but rather to issues having relevance to the choice of technical solutions within the framework of certain major principles.

Johansson examines three policy areas, studying among other things the effect of the accumulation and dissemination of knowledge within the framework of the various commissions on political positions. Johansson makes no distinction between evaluation and other kinds of analysis. It is, however, not unreasonable to interpret a significant part of the accumulation and dissemination of knowledge discussed in the dissertation as evaluation. A considerable number of the analyses submitted to the commissions in the three policy areas have been concerned with conditions that followed various central government interventions.

In one of these areas, the Swedish system of financing higher education, he considers himself able to ascertain that the Social Democratic party then in power changed its position as a result of studies commissioned by the special commission investigating the social framework of education in the early 1960s. What these analyses revealed, to the surprise of contemporary observers, was that imbalances in the recruitment of students from different social backgrounds were primarily located in the transition from compulsory schooling to upper secondary studies. More significant effects would therefore be produced by investing in measures permitting children from working-class homes to continue their studies after compulsory school, than by influencing the economic situation of university students. This led to the shelving of the original idea entertained by the Social Democrats of introducing nonrepayable maintenance grants. In our terms we should refer to this as an instance of double-loop learning.

However, this is the only instance among the cases studied by Johansson of a change of position on a central issue resulting from the provision of new factual and theoretical material demonstrating that an earlier position was based on erroneous assumptions with respect to empirical circumstances. Furthermore, the commission investigating systems of financial aid for students some twenty years later (1985-87) does not provide a single example of anyone drastically changing his or her point of view on the basis of information emerging from the various inquiries (Johansson 1992).

In studies by two different commissions inquiring into the field of dental care, Johansson also feels able to maintain that the investigations conducted into the effects of different social factors on dental health had some considerable influence on the construction of a new system of dental charges, and this was also the case when a subsequent commission worked on changes to the system introduced some years previously. In these cases, however, the use of the results did not involve any change in fundamental objectives. It was not a case of the knowledge acquired leading to the rejection of central assumptions. The knowledge gained from various studies—among them some that may fairly unambiguously be regarded as evaluations—influenced the technical design of the system. In this respect, however, significant use was made of the results, as the technical construction of the system would have been different if the designers had not had access to the analyses utilized in the work of the commission. In the case of defense, the third area studied by Johansson, a similar pattern emerges. It is his opinion that the knowledge acquired may have led to positions being influenced with respect to minor matters, but hardly at all in the case of major issues.

The material at our disposal would therefore seem to indicate that the utilization of knowledge acquired through the mediation of the commission system only produces double-loop effects in exceptional cases. Unfortunately, our knowledge of other kinds of evaluations and other spheres of activity is severely limited due to the lack of studies.

However, indirect indications, too, seem to confirm that double-loop learning proceeding from evaluations, independent of the source of evaluation, very rarely takes place. In studies of policy formation in different areas, such as housing policy, energy policy, crime prevention, and so on, newly acquired knowledge resulting from individual evaluations is almost never referred to as a major explanation for changes of any significance.

Even though individual evaluations would not thus appear to induce political decision makers to question the basic preconditions underlying a certain policy, it may perhaps be reasonable to hypothesize that if evaluations and other studies of the fundamental assumptions underpinning a policy should demonstrate that these were untenable, then they might bring sufficient pressure to bear on the politicians to make them reexamine the policy. We have therefore considered it possible, not perhaps to demonstrate irrefutably, but nonetheless to present as a clear hypothesis the notion that various forms of double-loop learning practically never, or at the very least extremely rarely occur in relation to the adoption of fundamental policy positions in Sweden.

We would not, however, wish to exclude the possibility of long-term learning effects. In the first place, it is conceivable that a number of evaluations of the policies pursued within a given policy area may result over time in the question being placed on the political agenda in a way that it would otherwise not have been. It becomes an issue on which politicians are obliged to take action. Second, it is possible that in the long term certain kinds of knowledge may influence judgments as to whether various regulatory measures are operating as intended. A conceivable but as yet not particularly well substantiated hypothesis might be formulated in the following terms: a whole series of studies undertaken in the 1980s with respect to the effects of different regulatory measures in the energy sector may have influenced politicians in the 1990s in their judgment of what may or may not be feasible to achieve with the help of various regulations in, for instance, relation to the environment.

But we must not let these reflections veil a conclusion for which it would appear that we possess at least a certain amount of corroborative evidence: evaluations do not appear to lead to double-loop learning if we consider central policy-making processes at the level of the government and Parliament. The learning occurring at this level is therefore to a great extent single-loop in character and essentially takes place within the framework of the budget process. A study based on interviews with officials in agencies in ministries involved in the new budget process and submitting in-depth requests in 1990, whose appropriations were dealt with by Parliament in 1992, shows that in its proposals to Parliament the government often makes explicit references to evaluations, with the evaluations often appearing as a reason for various technical changes.[4] Naturally, it is impossible to know what may lie behind these explicit references. Counterfactual hypotheses are just as intractable in relation to a discussion of the utilization of evaluations as in other contexts!

In this sense the budget process is a continuous learning process—not the least for ministry officials. But was not one of the motives underlying the new budget process this kind of extension of the process itself? The question is whether the scope of the budget process has been extended in such a way that we are able to state that some of the learning taking place has a double-loop character.

We are therefore entitled to ask if we are able to find any examples of ministries reassessing fundamental positions within the framework of the budget process. Such examples may indeed exist, but they are certainly not easy to find. In the first place it would appear that ministries have completely neglected to request such information as might reasonably be expected to lead to such fundamental reassessments. The evaluations requested are to a great extent intended as an aid to adopting positions within the framework of the fundamental assumptions held by the various agencies (RRV 1990).

In the second place, we are able to establish, on the basis of a survey of a number of agencies, that it appears to be the case that even taking the budget process for the fiscal year 1991/92, which deals with the allocation of resources for the three years following 1 July 1992, no really fundamental reassessments have been considered in connection with the evaluations ordered by ministries within the framework of the budget process.[5] To take one of several examples, the National Board of Forestry submitted its in-depth budget request for this period in the autumn of 1991. But when a forestry commission was set up in 1990 to produce briefing materials for a reassessment of forestry policy as a whole, this was a matter viewed as entirely separate from the budget process about to get under way some few months later. The available evidence thus indicates that material capable of leading to fundamental reassessments is not produced within the framework of the budget process.

This means that there is now a good deal of evidence indicating that one of the intentions underlying the new budget process, namely the introduction of more fundamental issues into the budget process itself, has not been realized. This also implies that certain types of learning are absent from the budget process. But how are we to regard evaluations intended to help in adopting a position within the framework of fundamental assumptions? What do the ministries learn from them? In the first place we may ascertain that the prerequisites for learning have improved. It is the unanimous view of both ministries and agencies that the quality of various kinds of briefing materials, including evaluations, has improved. In the interviews we have conducted with various officials in the ministries, it is frequently claimed that learning has occurred.

Those evaluations intended for use in connection with decision making in agencies are also to a high degree put to actual use. This is a bold assertion to make this despite having to rely on rather insubstantial evidence consisting of the survey mentioned above and interviews conducted with agency representatives in conjunction with other studies. The close relationship between the roles of orderer and user found with regard to the use of evaluations in internal agency processes argues powerfully for the correctness of this conclusion.

On the other hand, this use would appear to be exclusively a question of single-loop learning. The reason for this is not that double-loop learning is excluded in principle. Even at agency level, where the fundamental task is given a priori, means are chosen on the basis of various fundamental assumptions. An example may serve to illustrate the line of reasoning. The Swedish Customs and Excise Department combats the illegal supply of narcotics in order to control the consumption of narcotics. These questions are raised at government and Parliament level as if limiting the physical supply of narcotics is a good way of reducing the consumption of narcotics. If the government and Parliament were to alter the activities of the customs service on the basis of studies demonstrating that changes in the system of legal sanctions would provide a better way of affecting the supply of illegal drugs, then this would be an instance of double-loop learning. But we might also speak of double-loop learning if the Swedish Customs Agency had, for instance, chosen to employ dogs as a central aspect of border control in the area of narcotics, only to change this policy if it were to be shown that the use of dogs was predicated on quite erroneous assumptions with regard to the behavior of smugglers (or dogs).

But the kind of double loop that might conceivably occur at agency level would also appear to be extremely elusive. A reason for this may be that when questions of strategy are at issue at agency level, these are referred to the central government. The limitations on the scope actually available for double-loop learning within agencies may well explain why such learning does not appear to occur at agency level.

In the above discussion we have only dealt with "the reason why" to a very limited extent. Why, then, are some evaluations made more use of than others? Why do they so seldom lead to the raising of fundamental questions? It has perhaps been possible to deduce from what is implicit in our text that in our view the explanation for differences in use and learning are to be sought in the fundamental conditions governing the operation of political and administrative processes. Before leaving the question of the extent to which learning follows evaluations we may indicate another kind of explanation embedded in a conclusion drawn by Premfors (1987) on the basis of a study of evaluation activities in nine agencies. Premfors considers himself able to ascertain that in cases where an evaluation fails to give a unequivocal answer as to whether a matter evaluated is "good" or "bad," then the shaping of an agency's endeavors will be shifted toward a learning perspective. Such a state of affairs may well depend on the fact that the "more open" the conclusions of an evaluation, the easier it will be to use it to shed light on the different problems found in a set of activities and thereby initiate discussion and a learning process.

Conclusion

In this chapter we have shown that a rather comprehensive infrastructure of evaluations has gradually taken shape in Sweden. We have also seen that different decision-making processes acquire evaluations from different sources. A conclusion that may be drawn from our examination of the extent to which evaluations lead to learning is that only in exceptional cases do evaluations appear to play a part in significant changes of orientation in policy. They take on a more significant role in relation to adjustments of course or the choice of technical solutions within the framework of existent fundamental policy decisions. They are key tools of single-loop learning.

Whether this will be regarded as a discouraging finding or one that may nonetheless be viewed with some satisfaction depends on the expectations entertained in this respect. If it is expected that individual evaluations will influence fundamental political decisions and produce significant shifts of view in relation to such matters as the proper degree of involvement of central government, goals that should be given priority, and the means to be adopted to achieve these goals, then disappointment will inevitably ensue. However, such a view is probably rooted in misapprehensions with regard to the character of political decision making. When fundamental policy decisions are at issue, fundamental values are confronted by uncertainties as to how reality is constituted and the way in which various initiatives might affect the achievement of ultimate goals. In this case it would be verging on the pretentious to expect individual analyses, which must of necessity leave many politically relevant questions to one side, to lead to any sudden political reorientation on the part of political decision makers. At more technical levels, the situation is different. In such contexts evaluations are well able to play an appreciable role—and much evidence would indeed seem to indicate that they do.

As mentioned previously, the differences found in use and learning may therefore be better explained by the fundamental conditions affecting the various decision-making processes and the administrative and political circumstances characterizing them. Perhaps the best way of obtaining more knowledge of how evaluations are used and how they contribute to learning might even be to study these decision-making processes instead of concentrating on the fate of the many evaluations fed into them.

Our discussion leads us to believe that some of the factors that may affect use and learning may be related purely to the differences between the decision-making processes involving Parliament and the government in the Swedish context. An explanation of this kind may be for instance that the very fact that Sweden has ad hoc mechanisms for fairly fundamental reassessments of policy orientation that work relatively well makes it more difficult to gain any learning benefits from introducing analyses relating to such fundamental reassessments into the more formalized budget process.

The first thing we ourselves may learn from the discussion of what can be learned from evaluations, therefore, is perhaps to entertain quite different expectations concerning the part evaluations can play in the three distinct decision-making processes to which we have related our discussion. The second is to focus our attention on the decision-making processes and their characteristics, even when discussing learning from evaluations.

Notes

1. With the exception of Foyer 1969, there have been few studies of this function of the system. However, Premfors 1983, is able to confirm the significance of social research in the commissions. The publication of Johansson 1992 means there is a study now available that to a certain extent discusses this function within the commission system. In his essay "Seven Observations on Evaluations in the Swedish

Political System," Evert Vedung provides an overview of some of the features of Swedish commissions under the enlightening heading "The Stakeholder Model in Practise: Ad hoc Policy Commissions." One of the features of the commission system pointed out by Vedung is that their results are always published, providing "testimony to the remarkable openness of the Swedish State policy-making system."

2. For a fuller description of the Swedish budget system see Sandahl 1993.
3. In addition to the present writer, who bore the main responsibility for the study, a number of colleagues at the National Audit Bureau also participated in the work, namely Ulrika Barklund, Ulf Bengtsson, Mona Blomdin, and Karin Edholm.
4. Draft version circulated within the Swedish National Audit Bureau.
5. Draft version circulated within the Swedish National Audit Bureau.

References

DSSB. 1984. *Promemoria om det Svenska Utredningsväsendet.* statsrådsberedningen. Stockholm, Sweden: DSSB.

Foyer, L. 1969. "The Social Sciences in Royal Commissions in Sweden." *Scandinavian Political Studies* 4: 183–203.

Johansson, J. 1992. *Det Statliga Kommittèväsendet - Kunskap, kontroll, Konsensus.* Edsbruk, Sweden: Akademitryck AB.

Meijer, H. 1956. *Kommittépolitik och Kommittéarbete.* Lund, Sweden: Gleerup.

Myrdal, G. 1934. "Finanspolitikens Ekonomiska Verkningar." SOU.

National Audit Bureau. 1992. "A Survey of One Hundred Swedish Evaluation." Stockholm, Sweden: National Audit Bureau.

Petersson, O. 1988. *Maktens Nätverk.* Stockholm: Carlssons.

Premfors, R. 1983. "Governmental Commissions in Sweden." *American Behavioural Scientist* 26, no. 5: 623–42.

———. 1987. "Utvärderingsverksamhet på Central Förvaltningsnivå." *Statsvetenskaplig Tidskrift.* no. 4.

Riksrevisionsverket. 1975. *Utvärdering av Försöksverksamheten med Programbudgetering.*

———. 1987. *Utvärderingar - Till Vad Och Hur Mycket.* (Author: Jan-Eric Furubo).

———. 1990. *Mot en Resultatorienterad Budgetprocess - en Genomgång av de Myndighetsspecifika direktiven i budgetcykel 1* (Dnr 1989:238. Author: Inger Rydén).

———. 1991. *Att Mäta Resultatanalysen - Vem Analyserar Vad, Hur Mycket Och på Vilket Sätt?* (Dnr 23-91-1736. Author: Jan-Eric Furubo).

Sandahl, R. 1993. "Connected or Separated." In *Budgeting, Auditing, Evaluating:*

Functions and Integration in Seven Governments, ed. A. Gray, W. Jenkins, and R. Segsworth. New Brunswick: Transaction Publishers.
SOU. 1985:40. *Regeringen, Myndigheterna Och Myndigheternas Ledning.* Huvudbetänkande från verksledningskommittén Stockholm: Liber.
Statskontoret. 1991. Draft version of paper about the Swedish commissions.
Vedung, E. 1992. "Seven Observations on Evaluation in the Swedish Political System." In *Advancing Policy Evaluation: Lessons from International Perspectives,* ed., J. Mayne, M.L. Bemeelmans-Videc, J. Hudson, and R. Conner. Amsterdam: Elsevier Science Publishers.
Wikberg, S., and U. P. Lundgren. 1980. *Att Värdera Utbildning.* Stockholm: Wahlström & Widstrand.
Wildavsky, A. 1986. *Budgeting.* New Brunswick, NJ: Transaction Publishers.

3

Policy Evaluation and the Netherlands's Government: Scope, Utilization, and Organizational Learning

Frans L. Leeuw and Piet J. Rozendal

In recent years the budget of the Netherlands's government has come to approximately NLG (Netherland Guilder) 200 billion annually. Almost 25 percent of this amount is used to finance the national debt, leaving a little over NLG 150 billion for general administration and the implementation of all other government tasks, programs and services. The question of how effectively this money is spent is an important one for the management of the civil service, Parliament, and the Dutch citizen. In order to address this question data have to be systematically collected and analyzed.

Research can serve to establish whether a policy has had the intended effect and also to determine whether it has had any undesirable side effects. After all, neither those who make policy nor those who implement it can directly observe all its significant intended and unintended effects. One important instrument that can afford central government insight into the way in which policy is implemented and into its effects is policy evaluation research. The aim of this research is not only to obtain insight, but also to adjust, amend, or terminate policy or programs by utilizing study results.

We define policy evaluation research (or studies) as investigations of an empirical nature focusing on the implementation, effects and/or side effects of policy programs and policy instruments,[1] including services, as well as investigations that assess organizational effectiveness.

Theoretical Framework

A large part of public expenditure is devoted to influencing trends and processes within society. It is the duty of ministerial management to be aware of the extent to which their own policy is successful in this respect and, where possible, to make use of the findings to stimulate learning. This requires knowledge about the efficiency and effectiveness of public policies and their related expenditure of public funds. Ministerial management can best acquire this insight by conducting policy evaluation studies or contracting them out and by being involved in these activities.

According to Rist (1990) there are two parts to this involvement: one is "management by evaluation" and the other is "management of evaluations." In management by evaluation, ministerial management ensures that policy evaluation studies contribute to achieving the following three goals (Chelimsky 1985; Rist 1989). First, policy evaluations can be used for the purposes of preparing and implementing policy programs or instruments. A policy may be adjusted on the basis of evaluation results if its implementation is not proceeding according to plan, goals are not being achieved, or undesirable side effects are being experienced. Second, policy evaluation studies can also affect the budget. Changes made to policy on the basis of evaluation study results may have financial consequences and necessitate adjustments to the budget. Evaluating the effectiveness of programs and instruments can help in setting priorities and to justify the allocation of funds. Third, policy evaluation may also be useful in accounting for action, not only within the official body concerned but also to Parliament and the public. The advantage of policy evaluation in this type of situation is that the process of rendering accounts takes place on the basis of methods of collecting and analyzing data that can be checked by third parties.

Organizational Learning and Utilization of Evaluation Research

When policy evaluation results in showing a match or mismatch of results of policy programs or instruments to the goals or a mismatch of outcomes to expectations, and this is detected by the organization involved in the evaluation, single-loop learning is occurring. When evaluations result in limited changes to policy or in establishing priorities for program expenditure without the underlying "policy theory" being discussed (Chen 1990; Leeuw 1985, 1991a), then also single-loop learning takes place. If, however, evaluations lead to the amendment of the assumptions on which a policy is based (i.e., the policy theory) to a fundamental change in policy objectives or to a fundamental change of the system by which an organization's policy is made accountable, then double-loop learning occurs. In order to initiate single- and double-loop learning processes, the results and recommendations of policy evaluations must be exploited and it is here that the management of the ministries can play an important role.[2]

Management of Evaluations

Next to the management by evaluation, the other form of management involvement in policy evaluation studies is that management directly or indirectly controls the initiation, implementation, and completion of the study and ensures that the policy evaluation studies are used in an adequate and efficient manner. This "management of" responsibility is expressed in, among other things, provisions for initiating, implementing, and completing policy evaluations. One prerequisite for ensuring that policy evaluation studies are implemented efficiently, used where necessary, and thus contribute to the efficiency of the civil service, is that they be initiated, implemented, and completed in a planned fashion. This means that evaluation activities must be institutionalized to some degree. Institutionalization ensures the creation and maintenance of provisions and procedures for determining progress within and between the various units responsible for initiating, implementing, completing, and utilizing policy evaluation studies. Institutionalization is important for the following reasons:

1. It can ensure that policy evaluations are not carried out only sporadically. Derlien (1990) concluded, on the basis of a comparative study in eight industrialized countries, that institutionalization was necessary for the structural implementation of policy evaluation studies.
2. It is important for the learning capacity in ministerial organizations. This applies to both single-loop and double-loop learning. Organiza-

tions cannot arrive at a systematic form of learning if there are no provisions and procedures to ensure regular policy evaluation studies with internal quality assurance. If policy evaluation is not embedded in the infrastructure to some degree, utilization, and consequently organizational learning, will take place only incidentally.
3. Policy evaluation studies carried out internally as well as studies commissioned use public funds. Institutionalization is an instrument for promoting more efficient implementation of evaluation activities (Van der Doelen and Leeuw 1991).

Research Questions

The study discussed here addresses the following questions:

- To what extent are policy evaluation studies conducted within the Dutch central government, that is, within the thirteen ministries?
- What kind of management provisions are available to enable such studies to be conducted successfully?
- How do Dutch civil servants define utilization of policy evaluation research?
- To what extent are the findings and recommendations of policy evaluation research indeed used by civil servants, but also by ministers and Parliament?
- To what extent is there single- or double-loop learning occurring when results are utilized?

By linking questions dealing with the extent to which evaluation research is carried out, the ways in which it is structured, the extent to which results are used, and the extent to which organizational learning occurs, we present a follow-up to a problem raised by Chelimsky in 1985. She is of the opinion that

> the problem of organizing the evaluation function so as to optimize the use of evaluation findings in public management looms very large....Has progress been made, for example, over the last 15 years in developing the infrastructure and evaluative information bases that were missing under the PBBS?...It is in this area of systematic and comprehensive organizational development of the measures, instruments and data bases needed by program evaluators that some of the biggest challenges for the future are likely to arise. (Chelimsky 1985: 21)

Earlier, Bunker (1978: 223) also focused on this topic and stated that "one cannot improve the prospects for utilization without adjust-

Policy Evaluation and the Netherlands 71

ing organization structures and procedures." We try to elaborate on these relationships, adding the perspective of organizational learning.

Methods of Collecting Data

Use was made of four distinct questionnaires developed, piloted, and applied by The Court of Audit. One related to the extent of policy evaluation studies conducted in eleven central government ministries in the period between 1987 and 1990, a second focused on the way in which these ministries had organized duties and procedures with regard to evaluations, the third addressed the discussions that took place with the most senior officials regarding the findings from evaluations, and the fourth examined the results obtained (utilization-focused). Most of the officials in these eleven ministries who work in the field of evaluation were contacted for the first two questionnaires.[3] The officials were also asked to produce written evidence in support of their answers to a number of questions. These were subjected to further examination. They mainly consisted of research program, model agreements for the purposes of contracting out research, and orders inaugurating committees or providing for research to be carried out.

The third questionnaire was discussed with the most senior officials within the sections of the organization examined. These were usually director-generals or their representatives. One of the aims of these discussions was to assess the accuracy and completeness of information obtained. The fourth questionnaire was used in order to obtain information about attitudes and practice of officials with regard to the utilization of findings from evaluation studies.

With regard to the focus on utilization, we also applied comparative text analysis on both the evaluation reports[4] as well as on written evidence indicating that use of the findings, conclusions, or recommendations was made. This evidence concerned official government documents, including "White Papers,"[5] interoffice communications within the ministries, and speeches given by the minister or higher civil servants.

Extent of Policy Evaluation Studies within the Dutch Central Government

The first topic of inquiry noted above focused on the extent to which policy evaluation studies are conducted within the Dutch central government. Data to address this issue were collected in every ministry except the Office of the Prime Minister and the Ministry of Defence. The eleven involved were the Ministry of Foreign Affairs (including Development Cooperation); the Ministry of Justice; the Ministry of Home Affairs; the Ministry of Education and Science; the Ministry of Finance; the Ministry of Housing; Physical Planning and the Environment; the Ministry of Economic Affairs; the Ministry of Agriculture, Nature Management and Fisheries; the Ministry of Social Affairs and Employment; and the Ministry of Welfare, Health and Cultural Affairs. The number of policy evaluation studies conducted by or at the request of these ministries was examined. It further appeared that there was at least one section in each of the ministries that played a supporting or coordinating role in respect to evaluation. In all, seventy-four organizational units were involved: sixty-two research, advisory, or policy units at the level of the director-general as well as twelve organizational units directly reporting to either the Permanent-Secretary or the Minister.[6]

The seventy-four units involved in policy evaluation studies provided Court of Audit with a total of 939 titles of studies carried out between 1987 and 1989. Approximately one-third of these studies were conducted internally, by the unit concerned or by another unit in the same ministry. Two-thirds of the studies were conducted externally, contracted out to an organization outside the ministry concerned. Table 3.1 shows how many policy evaluation studies were reported to the Court of Audit for each ministry.

The table shows that most studies were reported by units at the Ministry of Education and Science; the Ministry of Housing, Physical Planning and the Environment; the Ministry of Transport, Public Works and Water Management; and the Ministry of Welfare, Health and Cultural Affairs. These four ministries account for 63 percent or 596 of the 939 studies.

In previous studies of the efficiency and effectiveness of subsidies (Algemene Rekenkamer 1989; Leeuw 1992) and public information campaigns (Algemene Rekenkamer 1991b; Mei et al. 1991), it was found that a considerable proportion of the evaluation reports submitted by the ministries did not meet certain minimum requirements. We therefore examined the extent to which the reports in our sample could actually be regarded as policy evaluation studies. For this purpose, a

TABLE 3.1
Number of Internal and External Policy Evaluation Studies Reported to the Court of Audit between 1987 and 1989

Military	Internal Study	External Study	Unknown	Total
Foreign Affairs	15	2		17
Justice	35	8		43
Home Affairs	17	27		44
Education and Science	106	92	4	202
Finance	27	15		42
Housing, Physical Planning & the Environment	36	106		142
Transport, Public Works and Water Management	23	77		100
Economic Affairs	7	76		83
Agriculture, Nature Management and Fisheries	28	19		47
Social Affairs & Employment	7	60		67
Welfare, Health and Cultural Affairs	13	138		151

Source: Algemene Rekenkamer, Verslag 1990, Deel II: Beleidsevaluatie-onderzoek binnen de rijksdienst, Den Haag, 1991: 28.

random sample of 102 titles was taken. We then requested the ministries in question to submit these reports.

Eighty-nine reports were submitted and thirteen failed to appear. In ten cases this was because the study had not yet been completed. In three cases no reason was given. The reports received were assessed by reference to the following basic criteria:

1. the presence of a clear outline of the problems, the objectives and the format of the study;
2. based on empirical data;
3. reference to at least one of a number of elements, namely:
   - the extent to which policy is implemented according to plan;
   - the extent to which policy goals are achieved;
   - the extent to which the achievement of policy aims or the failure to do so is the result of the policy instruments employed; and
   - the effects and side effects of the policy.

Of the eight-nine reports assessed, thirty-four met these criteria in full and ten met them to such an extent that they could be deemed to be policy evaluation studies. These forty-four reports can be roughly divided into: eleven studies of policy implementation; twelve studies of the achievement of goals; and twenty-one studies of the effects and/ or effectiveness of policy. The other forty-five reports that were assessed in this study cannot be regarded as policy evaluation studies. The reports in question include progress reports and forecasts. The fact that these reports do not meet the criteria for policy evaluation studies does not necessarily mean that they are of a low standard. They may contain information that is useful in the pursuit of a particular policy, but do not allow the implementation, success, and/or effects of the policy to be assessed.

Extrapolating from this sample of eighty-nine reviewed reports, it may be concluded that in the period from 1987 to 1989 approximately half of the 939 reported studies can really be regarded as having been policy evaluation studies. Of the studies that met the requirements of Court of Audit, about 25 percent were internal and 75 percent were external. A larger percentage of the external studies than of the internal ones met the requirements.

Management Provisions for the Purpose of Policy Evaluation Studies

Here attention has been devoted to the following management provisions and procedures (Algemene Rekenkamer 1991a; Hoogerwerf and Zoutendijk 1991):

- For *initiation of evaluations*, data were gathered regarding the existence of procedures concerning the submitting of proposals for evaluation research, the use that is made of evaluation research programs, the commissioning of research and the existence of model contracts.
- For *implementation of evaluations*, data gathering efforts focused on recording the duties of the supervisors, the use of standardized contracts when work is contracted out, and determining who has authority when problems arise in a study that is in progress.
- For *completion of and follow-up to evaluations,* including the utilization of the findings, three key domains were studied. These were: procedures that guarantee that management (especially senior management) is involved in and agrees with the goals and methods of disseminating and transferring evaluation findings, conclusions, and recommendations; the mailing of evaluation reports both within central government and outside; and the filing of evaluation reports, including the "evaluation trail."

It was concluded that provisions for the entire process of initiating, implementing, and following up policy evaluation studies are available on a higher than average level at eleven of the total of thirty-nine directorates-general. These directorates-general are principally at the Ministry of Foreign Affairs; the Ministry of Transport, Public Works and Water Management; the Ministry of Economic Affairs; the Ministry of Social Affairs and Employment; and the Ministry of Welfare, Health and Cultural Affairs. If only external studies are taken into consideration, two directorates-general at the Ministry of Housing, Physical Planning and the Environment can also be included in this list.

For eight directorates-general provisions are almost nonexistent, while there are very limited provisions for the directorates-general of Higher Education, University Education and Secondary Education (Ministry of Education and Science) and the directorate-general for Rural Areas and Quality Assurance (Ministry of Agriculture, Nature Management and Fisheries). Thirteen directorates-general may be described as average in this connection, while the remaining seven directorates-general are not at all involved in policy evaluation studies.

Utilization of Policy Evaluation Studies

The issue here is whether the results of policy evaluation studies can help make organizational learning occur and help make policy and the organization of central government more effective. If the answer is to be found, policy evaluations have to be examined for the role they play in influencing policy and budgets and in the process of accountability (Chelimsky 1985; Rist 1989). We also made the assumption that use could be documented. Therefore, in its government-wide audit on the functions of policy evaluation within the central government, the Algemene Rekenkamer focused on demonstrable, recorded use.

The utilization of findings, conclusions, and/or recommendations depends on, among other things, context. Context can be described as the environment in which evaluation studies are initiated, implemented, and followed up. The amount of experience that ministries have with such studies and the number of management provisions there are for conducting them or having them conducted will possibly influence the degree to which findings and/or recommendations are utilized. One influential consideration is that these organizations are experienced with the handling of evaluation research findings (Mulder et al. 1991).

Views on Utilization

It appeared that 55 percent of the officials interviewed in units where policy evaluation studies are conducted believed that the recommendations of almost all evaluation studies known to them had been incorporated into policy. Approximately 25 percent more thought that this had been the case in over half the reports. Thus, over 80 percent of people questioned said that demonstrable use had been made of results, conclusions, or recommendations. This positive view of utilization was reinforced by officials involved in the forty-four policy evaluation studies discussed earlier and selected by the Algemene Rekenkamer for further scrutiny. Eighty percent of them felt that there was written evidence of utilization with regard to these reports. Government officials were also questioned with regard to when, in their perception, utilization took place. The respondents were all working within units involved in (coordinating) policy evaluation research within the Dutch ministries; they were usually study directors of the projects.

From table 3.2 (below) it can be concluded that most of the respondents have a rather instrumental view on when utilization takes place. The findings presented in this table can also be interpreted in terms of both forms of organizational learning. We conclude that only item number 9 ("when policy goals are modified according to the findings of the evaluation studies") and item number 12 ("when the policy evaluated is terminated") can be labeled as examples of double-loop learning. Items 3, 7, 11, and 13 might cause double-loop learning to occur, but this is dependent on the contents of the evaluation findings themselves.

It should be stressed that till now only testimonial statements dealing with utilization have been discussed. Therefore, we now turn to actual, demonstable utilization.

Reports Examined

In order to subject officials' predominantly positive views of the utilization of evaluation studies to further scrutiny, forty-four evaluation reports (already referred to) were selected and assessed on the basis of whether there was any solid written evidence of the utilization of results, conclusions, and/or recommendations contained therein. Two of the forty-four reports ("Introduction of the New Joint Regulations Act" and "Assessing Old Age Policies") were not assessed for utilization

TABLE 3.2
Views on Utilization of Evaluation Studies

Item	Frequency
Utilization of evaluation studies take place during the following situations:	
1. When the findings are translated into operational terms on behalf of the formulation of policy documents, the budget, or when these findings are discussed within seminars or workshops	1
2. When findings from evaluation studies lead to modifications of regulations, budgets, organizational arrangements, or when evaluation results lead to changes in the government information about the policy evaluated	24
3. When new perspectives/views on the goals aimed at are formulated on the basis of evaluation studies	2
4. When implementation problems are diagnosed or when bottlenecks are passed by due to the utilization of evaluation findings	7
5. When recommendation are taken into account when the policy evaluated is modified	16
6. When evaluation results lead to a more professional attitude of policymakers and/or implementators	3
7. When the results lead to a debate with stakeholders that were not yet involved in the policy discourse	3
8. When evaluation studies increase the level of (political) consensus between ministries and Parliament in order to better implement the policy evaluated	2
9. When policy goals are modified according to the findings of the evaluation studies	1
10. When (within a short period of time [less than three months]) the responsible minister presents his/her reaction on the evaluation study and also informs Parliament about this reaction	2
11. When new policy initiatives that aim at trying to reach the policy goals already set are discussed	1
12. When the policy evaluated is terminated	1
13. When the political agenda is changed on the basis of findings from evaluation studies	1

Note: The total number of respondents was sixty-one. As respondents could give more than one answer to this question, the number of answers is not comparable with the number of respondents.

Source: R. Venderbosch, Internal mimeographed research document, Algemene Rekenkamer, Den Haag, n.d.

as they formed part of an incomplete series of studies for which no completion date was available.

In view of the population from which the random selection was made (all 939 studies reported by the ministries) the reports are representative only of the situation in the Dutch central government as a whole.

78   Can Governments Learn?

The Context of Utilization

We have already discussed the management provisions for initiating, implementing, and following up policy evaluation studies for the various directorates-general. In examining the follow-up to policy evaluation studies, we focused on the way in which recommendations were drawn up and finalized and at the level at which decision making on the report took place.

The way in which recommendations are formulated is important for the use that can be made of a study. Recommendations may indicate the direction in which policy should be adjusted. The way in which recommendations are formulated varies widely from ministry to ministry. In many cases this takes place at a relatively low level within a ministry. Recommendations are often then finalized at the level of the minister (and the minister's advisers) and/or the heads of the policy or research department.

We have also examined the question of which was the highest management level at which decision making on evaluation study reports took place. This question could be answered in the case of thirty-four reports and the information is based on the interviews with project directors. For thirteen reports decision making took place at the level of a policy or research unit; for six reports it took place at the directorate-general level; and for twelve reports at the level of the minister or the minister's advisers. With regard to three reports, decision making took place at the level of the project director. The interviews also made clear that with regard to only twenty-three of the thirty-four reports were the results of the decision making confirmed in documents.

Evidence of the Utilization of Policy Evaluation Studies

With regard to thirty-four of the forty-two reports, the respective ministries provided the Court of Audit with material that, in their view, provided clear evidence of the utilization of the findings and recommendations of the policy evaluation study in question. We examined whether this was, in fact, the case. In order to do so, the texts of the material provided by the ministries were compared and their contents analyzed. In addition, we examined who had used the reports, which sections of the reports they had used, and when and for what purpose they had been used.

TABLE 3.3
Purpose for which the Report Was Used

Use	Number of Reports
Exclusively focused on the support of the policy evaluated	4
Focused on amendments to policy or part thereof, namely: small amendments (8) major amendments (3) both (5)	16
Exclusively focused on the support of the organization responsible for the execution and implementation of the policy	14
Focused on changes of a part of the organization, namely: small changes (2) major changes (2) both (2)	6
Focused on the preparation of the annual budget	10

Source: Algemene Rekenkamer, Verslag 1990, Deel II: beleidsevaluatie-onderzoek binnen de rijksdientst (Algemene Rekenkamer: Den Haag, 1991).

We listed the parties who could have used the report. The groups of users can be categorized as follows: Parliament, ministers, and civil servants. Twenty of the forty-two reports were shown to have been used by one or more of the above categories of user. Evidence of the use of nine reports is shown in parliamentary documents that contain questions on the reports, for example. In addition to information provided by the officials involved in the selected studies, information from the databases of the parliamentary computer center (PARAC) was used, which includes all "White Papers" as well as parliamentary debates. However, with respect to one of these nine reports the use implied only the announcement that a reaction with regard to the report was in the making. In eleven cases evidence of use was found in documents in which the minister concerned had made his or her standpoint known. In all twenty cases the studies were also used by civil servants. Table 3.3 discusses the various uses of the reports.

The twenty reports were used to support the policy evaluated in general or in more specific terms. This indicated that the findings supported the activities implemented to realize the policy goals. Four reports were exclusively used to support the policies, while the other sixteen were also used to amend elements of the policies. Small amendments implied that only a limited part or an element of the larger policy was changed on the basis of the evaluation study without amending the policy sui generis. Next, all twenty reports were used to support the organization responsible for the execution and implementation of the policy. In ten cases reports were also used in the preparation of the annual budget.

It also appears that only a few reports focus on bringing about major changes to policy itself or to the organization responsible for the implementation. Three of the reports have suggested major amendments to both policy content and organizations. The extent to which single- or double-loop learning has occurred in these three cases is now discussed.

Single- or Double-Loop Organizational Learning: Three Case Studies[7]

The first study evaluated the effects of the transformation of several different provincial organizations in the field of labor circumstances, safety, health, and welfare into one integrated provincial organization (Jakobs and van Poucke 1989). The study aimed at giving insight into the question of how this transformation process has proceeded, and to what extent the goals were achieved. The study was commissioned by the Ministry for Social Affairs and Employment. It focused on one province (Gelderland). One of the goals of the project was to learn on behalf of future re-organizations within other provinces.

Content analysis of "White Papers" and other governmental documents in which use was made of this study indicate that important recommendations were presented that matched the already outlined policy idea of transforming and integrating different organizations into one. Utilization primarily referred to logistic and technical aspects of this organizational change without paying attention to a discussion of the goals of the 'new' organization or indicators to be used to assess its (future) effectiveness. We conclude that this case can be seen as an example of single-loop learning.

The second study (Operations Review Unit 1988) concerned the evaluation of the development program in the western province of Zambia. The program comprised some twenty projects relating to agriculture, health care, infrastructure, and institutional support. In these projects, different tools (Salamon 1989) were used such as grants and information programs. The aim of the evaluation was to establish the extent to which these projects were linked to one another, to examine program achievements and constraints, and to assess the program's future. A central issue was program sustainability. The study was commissioned by the Ministry of Foreign Affairs. Important recommendations of the evaluation concerned the following: (1) the continuation of financial and technical development assistance over a longer period of time in order to promote sustainable development; (2) the production of a development plan and strategy for the first three years; and (3) the professionalization of among others the (line) management of the Provincial Planning Unit. These and other recommendations (Operations Review Unit 1988: 13–15) were in line with the policy already developed and implemented, and were, generally speaking, accepted. The findings had an impact only upon the procedures already set into motion; they added neither a fundamental analysis nor a new perspective dealing with the goal achievement of this program. We therefore conclude that this case can be seen as an example of single-loop learning.

The third study concerned an evaluation of technology and applied technological research in the building and construction sector. It was commissioned by the Ministry of Economic Affairs (Moerdijk and Van Oosten 1988). The evaluation focused on the "IOP-instrument." (IOP stands for "Innovation-Oriented Research Programme.") IOPs were developed and implemented during the 1980s in fields like biotechnology, membrane technology, and the building and construction sector. They were aimed at medium- to long-term goals in the field of economic development and technology. The Moerdijk and Van Oosten evaluation concerned the building and construction sector. The main goal of this IOP was to stimulate research leading to technological innovations in the building and construction industry that in turn would lead to better cost-benefit ratios and to higher productivity levels in this sector. One conclusion of the evaluation was that there were "fundamental problems with establishing relationships between innovation oriented applied research on the one hand and the needs of industries in the field of the building of factories and houses." It was also concluded that as the need for research in these sectors is focused on short-term projects of a rather pragmatic nature, industry needs and the programming of IOP-activities drew apart. This and all other IOPs have primarily focused on medium- and long-term goals (Moerdijk and Van Oosten 1988). A third conclusion was that there had been rather large problems with respect to the organization and structure of the IOP.

It was concluded that this IOP therefore should not be continued but be terminated as of 1 January 1989. The Ministry of Economic Affairs agreed to this recommendation. Although for IOPs, in general, a life-period of eight years is planned, this IOP was terminated after only four years. "The evidence that the building industry appears not to have a strong need of applied oriented technological research but instead needs sector-oriented research has played an important role in reaching that decision" (Ministry of Economic Affairs 1988: 1).

The fact that the basic underlying assumptions about this IOP were addressed leads us to conclude that double-loop learning occurred. The basic underlying rationale of the IOP-instrument was openly examined and strongly criticized. The instrument appeared to be inapplicable in the building sector. This was caused by the discrepancy between, on the one hand, the medium- to long-term goals of the IOP-instrument and the rather short-term goals of the building sector on the other hand. The fact that the Ministry of Economic Affairs decided to terminate the application of this instrument half-way through its life stage was rather drastic.

Given the small number of cases, no general conclusions about conditions under which single- or double-loop learning occurs can be drawn. However, what our findings do show is that in one of the three cases of evaluation studies recommending major changes to policy and/or organizations, double-loop learning has taken place. This happened with regard to an evaluation study commissioned by the Ministry of Economic Affairs, which, as we discussed earlier, has an above average evaluation infrastructure.

Conclusion

Although the attention paid to policy evaluation research has increased over the years (Bemelmans-Videc 1989), the organization and infrastructure of evaluation studies within the central government are still rather limited. It appears that few ministries have an adequate system of arrangements and procedures for implementing evaluation studies efficiently and effectively.

In addition it has been established that twenty out of forty-two randomly selected evaluation studies (48 percent) could be shown to have been used explicitly. This did not tally with the considerably more positive view of the officials interviewed. In other words, there was no evidence of the use of over half the reports. This is open to both positive and negative interpretation. If one feels that each and every evaluation study should be used, then a figure of 48 percent is low. If one feels that the processes of policy, budgeting, and accountability encompass more than just using evaluation studies, then 48 percent is reasonable.

It should be noted that in establishing a criterion for use, we were extremely conservative—there had to be written demonstrable evidence of use for us to count it. Reports can also be used in other ways or by parties other than the three categories of users selected (Parliament, ministers, and civil servants). But these possibilities fell outside our definition and thus were not considered.

With regard to future research in the field of evaluation, utilization, and organizational learning, the following recommendations can be made. The first one deals with the role that the central government should play; the second and third concern the role of theory and methodology. Only half of the studies labeled by central government units as "policy evaluation studies" were indeed of this kind. When one takes into account that rather basic criteria were used to make distinctions, we believe it is necessary for the Dutch central government to increase the quality of its policy evaluation research. As of 1 January 1992, the Budget and Account Law has been expanded with a provision indicating that each minister is responsible for regularly performing policy evaluations in his or her department. In our opinion, it will be one of the roles of the Court of Audit to keep an eye on both the quality and the quantity of the evaluations performed.

The second recommendation focuses on the need to specify more precisely conditions under which single- and double-loop learning will occur. The question regarding the conditions under which decision makers strive for evaluation, knowledge utilization, and organizational learning should be central. What are the incentives for them to do so and what determines the working of these incentives? To answer this question, use can be made of work produced by rational choice theorists, elaborating on behavioral and institutional mechanisms determining information processing of government officials (Frey and Eichenberger 1991; Coleman 1990). Till now hardly any utilization study has made use of this social science tradition.

With respect to the third recommendation we believe it is necessary to improve on the measurement of utilization and learning. As one of us illustrated for Dutch applied sociology over the period from 1980 to 1990, there is "much more shoptalk about the utilization of social research than a meticulous investigation of specific types of utilization in conjunction with specific types of applied research" (Leeuw 1991b). We suggest investigators follow some of the more interesting examples of utilization research where text analysis is applied (Wingens and Weymann 1988; Mulder et al. 1991).

Notes

This chapter is partly based on a government-wide audit by the Algemene Rekenkamer published in its Annual Report 1990. In addition to the authors, the research team consisted of Hans-Paul Mulder, Guido Walraven, and Astrid de Groot of the Algemene Rekenkamer's Policy Evaluation Research Division. The authors wish to thank Ray C. Rist for his valuable comments on an earlier version.

1. We distinguish between policy programs (sets of policy activities addressing issues such as mental health, energy conservation, criminality) and policy instruments (tools of government, such as laws, subsidies, grants, loans, public information campaigns, etc.) (Salamon 1989). Programs can apply different tools, but tools are of a more fundamental nature because they refer to social and behavioral mechanisms that make programs "work."
2. It should be noted that Dery (1990: 24–25) is of a different opinion. He believes that the "prevailing notion of organizational learning . . . where program evaluation is seen as the means to test organizational theories [policies] and thus as a primary source of knowledge [for organizational learning] is at least partly incorrect." He argues that this notion of learning "holds that organizations are experimental entities. Knowledge utilization is thus expected, while non-utilization poses a crisis, or at least a problem that must be solved." In our opinion governmental organizations indeed are (or should be) "quasi-experimental entities," this the more so because the outputs of these bodies (policies) can be interpreted as solutions to problems that can be (partially) right or (partially) wrong and deserve testing (evaluation) (Albert 1977).
3. As there was no registration where to sample from, one of the first activities of the Algemene Rekenkamer was to develop such a list and subsequently interview most of the officials on that list. Only when there were several (more than five) officials working within the same unit, we restricted the questioning to one or two of them.
4. There were forty-four reports that were considered policy evaluation studies, but two were made to be assessed for utilization, as will be explained later in the chapter.

Policy Evaluation and the Netherlands 85

5. "White Papers" include: all the documents produced by the central government with a formal status and presented to Parliament; minutes of debates held in Parliament; and special reports produced by Parliament itself or by, for example, the Supreme Court or the Court of Audit.
6. It should be emphasized that policy evaluation studies are not conducted only by the instruction of the ministries. Activities are also carried out by the Social and Cultural Planning Office, the Central Planning Bureau, and the Scientific Advisory Council on Government Policy. None of these organizations, however, has been formally given the task of assessing government policy retrospectively.
7. This section is partly based on a mimeographed, unpublished document by H. P. Mulder and G. Walraven, "Notitie ten behoeve van de inbreng van de Algemene Rekenkamer in de IIAS-Working Group" ("Memorandum on behalf of input of the Algemene Rekenkamer to the IIAS-Working Group"), Policy Evaluation Division, Algemene Rekenkamer, 17 July 1991, Den Haag.

References

Albert, H. 1977. *Kritische Vernunft und Menschliche Praxis*. Stuttgart: J.C.B. Mohr Verlag.
Algemene Rekenkamer. 1989. *Verslag 1988*. Onderzoek naar subsidies. Den Haag, Netherlands: SDU.
———. 1991a. *Verslag 1990*. Deel II: Beleidsevaluatie-onderzoek binnen de Rijksdienst. Den Haag, Netherlands: SDU.
———. 1991b. *Voorlichtingscampagnes van het rijk*. Tussentijds Rapport. Den Haag, Netherlands: SDU
Bemelmans-Videc, M. L. 1989. "Dutch Experience in the Utilization of Evaluation Research: The Procedure of Reconsideration." *Knowledge in Society*. 2: 31–49.
Bunker, D. R. 1978. "Organizing to Link Social Science with Public Policy Making." *Public Administration Review* 38.
Chelimsky, E., ed. 1985. *Program Evaluation: Patterns And Directions*. Washington, DC: American Society for Public Administration.
Chen, H. T. 1990. *Theory-Driven Evaluations*. Newbury Park, CA: Sage Publications.
Coleman, J. 1990. *Foundations Of Social Theory*. Cambridge, MA: Bellknap Press.
Dery, D. 1990. *Data and Policy Change*. Boston: Kluwer Academic Publishers.
Derlien, H.U. 1990. "Genesis and Structure Of Evaluation Efforts in Comparative Perspective." In *Program Evaluation and the Management of Government: Patterns and Prospects across Eight Countries*, ed. Ray C. Rist. New Brunswick, NJ: Transaction Publishers.

Doelen, F. C. J. van der, and F. L. Leeuw. 1991. "Doelmatigheidsonderzoek Binnen de Rijksoverheid." *Beleidswetenschap* 5: 44–63.
Frey, B. S., and R. Eichenberger. 1991. "Anomalies in Political Economy." *Public Choice* 68: 71–89.
Hoogerwerf, A., and D. C. Zoutendijk. 1991. "Hoe Valt Het Evaluatie-On-Derzoek Zelf Te Beoordelen." In: *Beleidsevaluatie.* J.Th.A. Bressers & A.
Jakobs, J. J., and A.B.M. van Poucke. 1989. "Een Arbo-Dienst Aan De Arbeid; Evaluatierapport BGD Oost-Gelderland." Ministerie van Soziale Zaken en Werkgelegenheid (Ministry for Social Affairs and Labor). Den Haag, Netherlands: SDU.
Leeuw, F. L. 1985. "Population Policy in Industrialized Countries: Evaluating Policy Theories to Assess the Demographic Impact of Population Policy." *Genus* 41: 1–19.
———. 1991a. "Policy Theories, Knowledge Utilization, and Evaluation." *Knowledge and Policy* 4: 173–91.
———. 1991b. "Knowledge Transfer and Application in Dutch Sociology; Some Developments between 1980 and 1990." In *In Pursuit of Progress; Assessing Achievements in Dutch Sociology,* ed. H. A. Becker, F. L. Leeuw, and K. Verrips. Amsterdam: SISWO-Publishers.
———. 1992. "Government-Wide Audits In The Netherlands: Evaluating Central Government Subsidies." In *Advancing Public Policy Evaluation: Learning from International Experiences,* ed. J. Mayne, M. L. Bemelmans-Uidec, J. Hudson, and R. Conner. Amsterdam: Elsevier Science Publishers.
Mei, W. J. G. van der, P. J. Rozendal, F. L. Leeuw, and G. N. J. A. Bukkems. 1991. "Effecten van voorlichtings campagnes." *Openbare Uitgaven* 24: 192–204.
Ministry of Economic Affairs. 1988. Brief inzake Evaluatie IOP-Bouw (December). Den Haag, Netherlands.
Moerdijk, H., and J. van Oosten. 1988. *Evaluatie IOP—bouw over de periode 1983–1987.* Mijdrecht, Netherlands: Bureau Moerdijk & Van Oosten, Mijdrecht.
Mulder, H. P., et. al., 1991. "Gebruik Van Beleidsevalua Tie-Onderzoek Bij De Eijksoverheid." *Beleidsweten schap* 5: 203–228
Operations Review Unit. 1988. "Zambia Western Province." *Evaluation Report 1988.* Den Haag: Netherlands Development Cooperation.
Rist, R. C. 1989. "Management Accountability: The Signals Sent by Auditing and Evaluation." *Journal of Public Policy* 9: 355–69.
———. ed. 1990. *Program Evaluation and the Management of Government: Patterns and Prospects across Eight Countries.* New Brunswick, NJ: Transaction Publishers.
Salamon, L., ed. 1989. *Beyond Privatization: The Tools Of Government Action.* Washington, DC: The Urban Institute Press.
Wingens, M., and A. Weymann. 1988. "Utilization of Social Sciences In Public Discourse: Labeling Problems." *Knowledge in Society* 1: 80–97.

PART II

Institutional Perspectives

4

Organizational Learning at the U.S. Office of Personnel Management

John A. Leitch and Ray C. Rist

Federal agencies within the U.S. government have been increasingly involved in developing and using various "indicators" or "performance measures" as a means to track how well (or poorly) they are carrying out their assigned responsibilities. The U.S. General Accounting Office (GAO), the audit and evaluation arm of Congress, studied the Office of Personnel Management (OPM) to examine its development and use of organizational performance measures (GAO 1990). The examination addressed performance measures and standards for quality, efficiency, timeliness, and customer satisfaction. GAO looked at how widely OPM was covered by performance measures and standards, and how performance measures were reported to various management levels. In the context of the GAO study, a standard is a norm of performance and a measure is the evaluation of actual performance.

The examination resulted in describing a performance evaluation structure such as that needed for organizational learning. As pointed out by Leeuw and Sonnichsen in the introductory chapter, organizational learning is an iterative process through which an organization tries to become more competent in solving organizational problems and taking action. According to Argyris,

> Learning may be defined as occurring under two conditions. First, learning occurs when an organization achieves what is intended; that is there is a

match between between its design for action and the actual outcome. Secondly, learning occurs when a mismatch between intention and outcome is identified and corrected; that is, a mismatch intention and outcome is identified and corrected; that is a mismatch is turned into a match. (Argyris 1988: 541).

OPM's performance evaluation structure enables a comparison between intention and outcome. It consists of explicitly stated expected outcomes in terms of performance standards, evaluations of actual outcomes in terms of performance measures, and mechanisms for reporting the match or mismatch between expected and actual performance outcomes to management for appropriate action.

This case study discusses OPM's performance evaluation structure and its potential improvement through: (1) broadening the use of organizational performance measures and standards for quality, timeliness, and efficiency; and (2) better developing customer satisfaction information that could be used to challange existing standards for performance.

In addition to describing OPM's performance evaluation structure, this case study raises the issue of performance information needed for double-loop learning. Argyris and Schon (1978: 18–23) describe organizational learning as either "single loop" or "double loop." Single loop is described as determining mismatches between expected and actual outcomes and then making instrumental changes such as changing procedures or resourse levels in order to help meet an established organizational objective. Double loop goes beyond changing instrumental aspects to challenging and changing organizational policies and performance standards in order to meet an overall objective. Schon (1985: 119–20) points out that single loop learning connects detection of error to strategies for action while norms are held constant, whereas double loop learning connects to both strategies for action and to the norms by which actions are evaluated. This case study discusses the role of customer satisfaction performance information as a factor in changing norms for quality, timeliness, and efficiency, that is, creating the conditions for double-loop learning.

Finally, this case study discusses the organizational learning that is in process as a consequence of GAO's evaluation of OPM. OPM is altering its performance evaluation structure as a consequence of GAO's evaluation—in other words, organizational learning about its organizational learning system.

OPM Context and Organization

OPM is the federal agency with primary responsibility for federal work force issues. OPM is responsible for developing and setting policies and regulations for other federal agencies to follow in managing human resources.

OPM also provides a variety of services to federal agencies, individuals seeking federal employment, and 9 million federal employees, retirees, and their survivors. These services include providing information to, and examining the qualifications of, applicants seeking federal employment; training current employees; maintaining a health benefit program for employees, retirees, and their survivors; and establishing and making changes to annuity payments to retired federal employees.

OPM employs approximately 5,000 employees and is headed by a director who is appointed by the president. About 80 percent of the employees are involved in providing direct services and 20 percent are involved in policy and regulations issues. Services are provided through the headquarters and a service center located in Washington, D.C., and five regional offices located throughout the country.

OPM has four primary suborganizations, called groups, which are responsible for delivering the services mentioned above. GAO's examination covered three of these groups in their entirety, and the majority components of the fourth. A description of the groups and services follows.

Retirement and Insurance Group. This group administers the civil service retirement, health, and life insurance programs. Within the group, the retirement office develops legislation, policy, and regulations relating to federal retirement matters, as well as adjudicates retirement claims and provides related services to federal annuitants and their survivors.

The insurance office develops legislation, policy, and regulations relating to health insurance programs for federal employees and oversees the health insurance program. The health insurance program is actually carried out on a day-to-day basis by contractors, and the insurance Office has the responsibility of establishing and monitoring contracts for life and health insurance programs.

Career Entry and Employee Development Group. The Career Entry and Employee Development Group manages programs associated with hiring, such as recruiting, examining, and conducting special programs for veterans, minorities, and women. The Career Entry Group attempts to produce a pool of qualified applicants that reflects the diversity of American society. The Career Entry services include widely disseminating information on available federal jobs, providing instructions on how to apply for them, and examining job applicants.

The group also manages training programs for employees. The Office of Employee and Executive Development researches the education and training needs of the federal agencies and develops training courses to fulfill these needs. They also obtain instructors, either from within the federal government or through contactors.

Investigations Group. The Investigations Group is a nationwide operation that conducts background investigations of current or potential federal employees and federal contactors' employees. Investigations are conducted to determine an individual's suitability for employment and when necessary, determine individuals' trustworthiness for jobs requiring security clearances. Services provided to other federal agencies by the Investigations Group include a variety of in-depth background investigations of people applying for sensitive positions and limited investigations of suitability for normal employment.

Personnel Systems and Oversight. This group provides policy direction and leadership in developing, administering, and evaluating federal agencies' personnel systems. This was the group not entirely covered by GAO's examination. Within the Personnel Systems and Oversight Group, the GAO study focused primarily on the Office of Agency Compliance and Evaluation, which conducts reviews of federal agencies' personnel management programs and brings about corrective action in those programs when such action is indicated by the reviews. Agency compliance services include government-wide reviews of significant personnel trends, single agency reviews of personnel initiatives, and single location reviews of significant personnel problems.

As can be seen from the above descriptions, OPM customers include (1) individuals, as in the case of retirement claims; (2) federal agencies, as in the case of background investigations; and (3) the entire federal work force, as in the case of reviews of agencies' compliance with federal personnel regulations.

The GAO Context

GAO, in conducting its normal business, can influence a federal agency's organizational learning process. GAO's evaluation role in this and other studies results in it being the provider of feedback on an organization's performance against objectives, that is, identifying, in Argyris's terminology, a mismatch between intention and outcome. GAO's traditional role as the congressionally mandated auditor and evaluator of federal agencies requires that it examine the results and performance of many operations and programs. These evaluations cover operations ranging from major military operations entailing billions of dollars to programs of very small agencies and bureaus.

The primary reason for initiating a number of GAO evaluations is the evidence of, or perception that, certain objectives or expectations are not being met.[1] In particular, many GAO evaluations address efficiency and economy issues in the operation of federal agencies. Still other normative evaluations address potential discrepancies in meeting program objectives such as the failure of government social programs to deliver services in the way recipients and congressional oversight committees expect.

One of the first steps in GAO normative evaluations is the establishment of the criteria against which the organization or program will be examined. Criteria may be program expectations or objectives that are spelled out in law, regulations, budget submissions, or other formal statements. Criteria, when not spelled out by law or other formal documents, may be based on generally accepted management principles. In any event, program objectives, expectations, or criteria form the starting point for many GAO studies of federal activities.

GAO's studies generally end with recommendations on how to correct discrepancies between actual and expected program results. The recommendations may be given to Congress for legislative action or to the relevant executive branch agency for administrative action. By law, GAO cannot require that management act to improve; it can only recommend to the government agency or to Congress that particular actions be taken.

Structural Components of an Organizational Learning System

The GAO study discussed here is the first in a planned series of studies in which GAO expects to assess OPM's service to their customers. To begin the series, GAO wanted to determine what mechanisms OPM had in place that would enable management to evaluate performance in providing services—and to make corrections when service did not achieve expected norms. The examination covered OPM's ongoing system for evaluating performance in the four service units—those organizations involved in retirement and insurance programs, background investigations, career entry and employee development activities (recruiting and training), and evaluation of other agencies' personnel activities.

In setting the framework for this study, GAO asserted criteria for performance evaluation based on generally accepted management practices. These criteria are as follows:

- First, to help ensure that operations are properly managed and customers satisfactorily served, an organization needs performance measures and standards. A performance measure, such as the number of days required to process retirement claims, can be matched against a standard to determine if management's or customers' expectations are being met. Measures by themselves can identify whether performance is improving or declining by comparing to past periods.
- Second, a system of reporting performance measures is needed to provide managers with performance results in a form and format that facilitates decision making at all managerial levels. While first line managers need detailed performance measures to ensure that program objectives are being met and services are being appropriately provided to customers on a daily basis, top management needs summarized performance information to track overall mission achievement, identify problems, and hold first line managers accountable.
- Third, to assure that managers have the incentive and motivation to correct for differences (mismatches) between expected and actual performance, a system of accountability for performance must exist.

These criteria parallel the structure needed for an organizational learning system as suggested by Argyris (1988: 541). The structure is essentially one based on a feedback mechanism, that is, an identification of what should be the outcome of an organization's activity; it is a means to measure whether the actual outcome does or does not match the intended outcome, and a mechanism for reporting this match or mismatch back to the organization so that needed adjustments may be made.

The GAO study addressed the question of whether the above performance evaluation mechanisms existed and how OPM used appropriate measures and standards in assessing the quality, timeliness, and efficiency of services provided to customers. In that regard, the examination addressed the *structure* required for organizational learning. GAO did not, however, cover the issue of how well OPM used its own performance evaluation information for making changes to correct organizational or individual performance. For example, GAO did not study the outcomes of efforts made within OPM to change organizational processes or policies.

The GAO study focused on the specific services that OPM managers identified as being key to the successful accomplishment of their mission in each of the four service areas. To do this, we identified three things: (1) the key outputs and services of OPM's operational units and what performance measures and standards exist for these services; (2) what information is routinely provided to the various managerial levels, including the OPM directorate level, on the operational units' performance in delivering key services; and (3) how performance expectations and standards are used in OPM to hold managers accountable for results.

To determine which were key outputs among the many outputs and services of OPM, we asked the managers who were responsible for the four functions to identify the services that they believe are the most important to their customers, and thus the key services for judging the performance of their organizations (Mikalovich: 1990). Further, to identify available information on organizational performance in providing these key services, we asked managers to provide documentation on performance measures and standards that exist and are reported.

When asked to identify the key services of the units under their direct charge, they identified twenty-four services. GAO next asked for information on performance measures and standards for the twenty-four services, if available. OPM's managers were able to provide reports and other documents that showed that 76 percent of the measures and 36 percent of the standards—for quality, timeliness, efficiency, and customer satisfaction—had been developed for the OPM's key output services.

96   Can Governments Learn?

The Structure of OPM's Ongoing Systems for Evaluating Program Performance

In concept and design, OPM's systems for monitoring program performance in the four service units have all the parts of the organizational learning system suggested by Argyris (1988). In other words, in terms of OPM's performance evaluation systems, there are expectations, measures of actual performance against expectations, feedback, and decisions based on comparing actual to expected performance. GAO found that:

- OPM has performance measurement systems that rather completely capture quality, timeliness, and efficiency information. In only a few cases, however, is comprehensive customer satisfaction information obtained.
- Program expectations or standards are identified for many specific services by management. The expectations varied from being expressed in general terms for hard to measure programs to specific performance standards for repetitive, short cycle services.
- Accountability for performance in carrying out the programs is contained in performance contracts for senior executive service program managers, and in documented work expectations for other levels of management.

OPM performance measures and standards are in most instances quantitative. As an example of one such qualitative standard, Interim Retirement Annuity claims are to be completed in twelve to fourteen days and with no more than 4.5 percent errors. However, in some instances, specific quantitative measures may not always be easily developed or practical for OPM's services. In these situations, OPM is using alternative, qualitative measures and standards. For example, the standard for the Agency Compliance and Evaluation Office's Targeted Installation Reviews states that "Reports reflect full coverage of all compliance issues, specify violations and recommend appropriate corrective actions. Reports are written in clear language and are organized logically." Other organizations, when faced with similar situations, have developed alternative "checklist indicators" that suffice in lieu of more quantitative measures (Mali 1978: 99).

Feedback to management on actual performance is provided in a variety of documented forms. Performance for services requiring relatively short cycle operations is documented frequently, generally on a four-week basis. For example, a sample of completed investigations is taken every four weeks and the timeliness is measured and reported. Timeliness for investigations is defined in terms of meeting promised dates. The percentage of cases meeting promised dates is the reported measure, and a goal (currently 80 percent) is annually established. Inspection group reports contain timeliness, quality, and efficiency performance information in one single report.

Many of the reporting systems are structured to enable management to readily identify discrepancies between expected and actual performance, thus setting the stage for inquiry into the sources of the error, decision making, and error correction actions that are an integral part of organizational learning (cf. Argyris and Schon 1978: 19).

In the case of the investigation's function, for example, the reports show the standard for timeliness next to each region's timeliness performance for each four-week period and for the year to date. Such reporting enables management to easily examine the performance information, identify mismatches, and take action to adjust procedures or improve processes. In another example, the retirement function measures timeliness and efficiency of processing annuity claims on a four-week basis. Performance measures for this service and several others are contained in a single report that also identifies the performance standards. The reports are distributed to the program manager and lower-level supervisors. Quality is measured on both a four-week basis and quarterly. The quarterly evaluation is performed by an independent OPM quality assurance function, and a detailed audit report is prepared and provided to the program manager and higher levels of management within the Retirement and Insurance Group.

In sum, OPM's evaluation system has a design that, if fully implemented, permits management to evaluate performance and use such evaluations in organizational learning. A performance evaluation properly designed for organizational learning would contain the key parts of a such a system. This would include measures of actual performance, standards or expectations against which to judge performance, and adequate reporting to allow all management levels the opportunity and ability to make informed judgments about actions necessary to correct discrepancies in performance.

98   Can Governments Learn?

OPM's Capacity to Evaluate Itself: Weakness in the Evaluation System

Although the GAO study showed that while OPM has the basic structure in place to sustain continuous performance monitoring, OPM's capacity to evalute itself and use the evaluation results for organizational learning is limited. This is because:

- Many potential measures and standards have not been developed. Each of the twenty-four services could potentially have four standards (timeliness, quality, efficiency, and customer satisfaction) and a measure for each. With four standards and four measures for each of the twenty-four services, there are a possible ninety-six performance standards and ninety-six performance measures for the key services. GAO's review showed that seventy-three (76 percent) of the total potential measures and thirty-five (36 percent) of the possible standards have been developed.
- Measures and standards are missing primarily in the efficiency and customer satisfaction areas. Slightly more than half (thirteen of twenty-four) the potential measures of efficiency exist for the 24 services, and only one of the twenty-four services—background investigations—has an efficiency standard. There are no performance standards for customer satisfaction for any of the services.
- Reporting of many performance measures is limited. For example, the Retirement Group managers have attempted to obtain customer satisfaction data from a customer survey and from retiree correspondence. However, the data are not systematically collected, hampering any potential analysis. The customer survey form is available only to those who happen to see it in the rack and choose to complete it, in contrast to being uniformly provided to all or to a statistically valid sample of customers.
- Performance feedback reporting is not provided to higher levels of management. OPM's top management regularly receives only limited performance reports from operating units. Performance reporting is generally kept within the functional units. Detailed measures are reported to the first line operation managers, and summarized performance reports are prepared for program managers. However, performance reports to the directorate level are limited to a few on a regular basis.

Utilization of Performance Evaluation Information

As previously stated, our work did not directly address either the issue of how well OPM used evaluations to improve performance, or the management actions involved in deciding what improvement course to take. However, in the course of the study, we collected some examples of managerial action to correct disrepancies between expectations and actual outcomes. These, for the large part, were examples of action on the instrumental level—changes in processes and procedures. Since these actions did not result in changes to performance standards or strategies, they indicate that organizational learning in these cases was single-loop in nature.

For example, federal agencies needing employees with security clearances complained that OPM's background investigations were taking too long. Investigation program management had initially established timeliness standards for the process, but had not been meeting these standards on a consistent basis. Many of the customer agencies had hired personnel with the expectation that these individuals would be put to work relatively close to the times set by OPM's standards. However, because OPM had delays in completing the background investigations reports, customer agencies often lost productivity because their employees could not be asigned promptly to planned sensitive work. OPM's primary action in this case was to hire more investigators, rather than to change the process or form of investigation. The result has been that processing times are shorter, but still do not meet customer needs.

Another example of single-loop learning is the action taken to speed enrollment changes in the Health Benefits program. In that program, enrollees are permitted to switch from one insurance plan to another once a year. The period for switching, called the "open season," occurs in late November and early December each year. OPM has a performance standard that the changes must be processed by 1 January of the next year.

Each individual agency processes changes for their current employees and OPM processes changes for retirees. In the past, OPM had difficulties achieving the 1 January milestone. In order to achieve the milestone, management decided to hire a contractor to computerize the process, and to have the contractor operate the processing system. Although the standard is not totally achieved, significant improvements have been made in timeliness with the new process.

In the above examples, actual performance is generally judged against norms or standards that have been established by management. In setting norms or standards, management may use its best judgment of what the customer requires, but often may not carefully derive input from the customer in making such judgments. As was noted earlier, only a few OPM services are measured in terms of customer satisfaction. This limitation deprives OPM of an important feedback tool. As pointed out by Michael, if demand for a type of product or service has changed, an organization will not know that fact without continuously testing with some sort of "environmental sensor" (Michael 1981: 259).

By not obtaining customer input when establishing operational norms or standards, management can cause itself future problems. For example, performance against internally set timeliness, efficiency, and quality goals may be achieved, and the organization rolls merrily along, blythly ignorant of the fact that it is not performing in a manner that is needed to meet the most important goal—customer satisfaction. This may not be entirely intentional ignorance, since meeting customers' satisfaction is one goal that calls into question the managerial judgment and performance regarding policies, procedures, products, and management approaches—and management may be reticent to have its judgment questioned (Pucik, 1988: 86).

It appears that OPM has the problem noted in the introductory chapter in this book; namely that the incorporation of information into a decisionmaker's knowledge base is *selective*. Selective information in OPM focuses on timeliness, efficiency, and quality as perceived by management. Yet management has limited means for determining if the performance expectations they have established are the right ones because they have little customer satisfaction measurement data. Without systematic customer feedback, OPM cannot tell if it is doing the right things, whether the right performance is being measured, or if it has the right performance expectations and standards. There appears to be "distancing," as described by Argyris (1988: 547), which prevents management from engaging in double-loop learning.

In the GAO study, one example of double-loop learning was noted. Here the "distancing" problem appears to have been overcome by outside pressures directly from the customers and through Congress. The Retirement Office received many complaints from retiring federal employees and from Congress about poor timeliness. Primarily, complaints addressed inordinately long times required between the day of a person's retirement from active service until the first retirement check arrived. Although the timeliness standard was sixty days, the actual processing time was often three or four months. Much of the time for processing the claims was taken up by collection of information after OPM received the claim for an annuity. For example, in certain cases, spouses have to be contacted to insure that they understand the terms of the retirement annuity being selected. Mailing forms to the spouse to review and sign takes time, but must be done to protect the spouse's equity.

In considering ways to reduce processing time, OPM determined that it could make an early estimate of the value of the total annuity soon after receiving the claimant's paperwork. OPM decided to change its policy of waiting until a claim is fully completed before paying an annuity. It determined it should process a partial claim as quickly as possible based on that initial determination, and to provide the retiree an estimated annuity check within fourteen days. The full annuity payment would start later and would include any appropriate adjustments. This approach has been adopted and the fourteen-day norm is regularly achieved. The decision by OPM to change both an organizational policy and a performance standard constitutes double-loop learning.

Leeuw and Sonnichsen pointed out in the "Introduction" to this volume that policy and program evaluation is not likely to effectively promote organizational learning unless it is accompanied by an environment that encourages utilization. They state that in order to ensure that program evaluation "play[s] a systematic instead of an ad hoc role in the process of organizational learning, an environment should be created which encourages the efficient and timely performance of evaluations as well as the utilization of its results."

As previously described, OPM's performance evaluation system was limited in providing efficient and timely performance measures. Further, the lack of reporting of performance measures to higher management levels may have hampered the utilization of evaluation results. This suggests the existance of an environmental problem such as noted by Leeuw and Sonnichsen. In this regard, the next section describes a change in the environment toward one that encourages utilization.

Utilization of GAO Evaluation by OPM

As can be seen from the preceding discussion, the structure of OPM's evaluation system has limitations. Hence, OPM's ability to evaluate its performance is called into question by GAO (see GAO

1990: 3–9). GAO's evaluation of OPM concluded with recommendations to the director that she establish a more comprehensive and strategic approach to the development and use of performance measures and standards. In particular, GAO suggested that the performance information system should entail: (1) determining who are the customers, what are the key services provided to those customers, and developing performance measures for those customers; and (2) developing a performance reporting system that has the flexibility to focus on differing services' performance and reporting to various management levels as needed.

Through the process of GAO's presentation of the findings, OPM senior management became concerned with weaknesses in the way they were managing the organization. They are now acting to correct it. The steps in this process have been as follows:

1. GAO provided a series of three briefings to OPM's top management, including the OPM director. All program heads were in attendance at the final briefing.
2. The OPM director issued a directive to the program managers to use the GAO methodology to determine what measures should be developed for assessing program performance.
3. The OPM director requested that the Office of Policy begin to establish a performance reporting system that would provide selected key information regularly to the directorate level.
4. The program managers have completed the first steps of developing performance measures by reconfirming their initial assessment of who were their customers and re-evaluating key measures of performance for serving those customers.
5. The program manager of the group with the largest two programs has initiated an effort to develop customer satisfaction measures. Customer satisfaction information is now being formally collected for the retirement program. A periodic survey is now conducted that obtains customer perceptions of the timeliness, courtesy, and competence of the service.

OPM's director, who had been in the job less than one year, began these actions to improve the environment for utilization of the evaluation information. In particular, she strengthened the accountability for action to improve performance and thus increased the use of performance information in managerial decision making. She also began centralizing the reporting of key performance information, which had been performed mainly at the program level (and which had previously left top management without the information to regularly ap-

The U.S. Office of Personnel Management 103

prise operational performance). Selected key performance information is now provided on a regular basis to the director.

As a consequence of these steps, organizational learning is occurring regarding OPM's organizational learning system, that is, the performance information system. As stated by Argyris and Schon, "organizational learning might be understood as the testing and restructuring of organizational theories of action" (1978: 11). OPM had a particular theory-in-practice (the actual processes, procedures, and actions of the organization in operating its performance information system). The OPM theory-in-practice regarding its program performance information systems appears to have been to collect quantitative program performance measurement information, but report and use the data at lower and mid-management levels. Top management was informed of program performance through other means. Another aspect of its theory in practice was to obtain customer feedback through informal contacts with customers. This theory-in-practice is now being changed to match an espoused theory-of-action (the new director's formally stated requirements for processes, procedures, and policies in operating OPM's performance information system).

If the prior policy regarding the performance information system was the same as that espoused by the new director, then single-loop learning is occurring. That is, the director is merely restating the policy or theory-of-action and mismatches between policy objectives and actual policy implementation are being corrected. However, if the director's policy is new and improved over the old policy, then implementing the new policy constitutes double-loop learning.

However, we do not know if single- or double-loop learning is occuring as OPM changes its performance information system. This is because we do not know if, prior to GAO's study, OPM had a formally stated policy based on a formally developed rationale (espoused theory) that described the structure and use of its performance information system. If there had been such a policy, then the performance information system now being instituted could be normatively compared to the prior policy to determine if single-loop learning was occurring (action taken to bring the system into conformity with existing policy). Double-loop learning could also be occurring. We simply do not have the data to address this issue.

Conclusion

In sum, the evidence and analysis presented here suggests that organizational learning is occurring in OPM. The dominant form of that learning appears to be single-loop, though at least one instance of double-loop learning has been documented. But what is also clear is that organizational barriers exist that can inhibit further learning. The present system may well work against double-loop learning, for it is not clear that there is systematic effort underway to reexamine and study basic goals and objectives of the organization. There will also be hinderance of single-loop learning so long as basic measurement issues are not resolved. But as in all learning processes, what is described here is just that—a process. And the fact that this process is underway has to be encouraging to all those who care about quality in the public sector.

Notes

The views expressed here are those of the authors and no endorsement by the United States General Accounting Office is intended or should be inferred.
1. This is frequently referred to as a normative evaluation where the existing condition is measured against a standard or criteria (see Rist 1985, 1992).

References

Argyris, C. 1988. "Problems in Producing Usable Knowledge for Implementing Liberating Alternatives." In *Decisionmaking: Descriptive Normative, and Prescriptive Interactions,* ed. David Bell, Howard Raiffa, and Amos Tversky. Cambridge, England: Cambridge University Press.
Argyris, C., and D. Schon. 1978. *Organizational Learning: A Theory of Action Perspective.* Reading, MA: Addison-Wesley.
Mali, P. 1978. *Improving Total Productivity: MBO Stragegies for Business, Government, and Not-for-Profit Organizations.* New York: John Wiley and Sons.
Michael, S. R. 1981. "The Control Cycle." In *Techniques of Organizational Change,* ed. Michael R. Stephen, Fred Luthans, George Odiorne, W. Warner Burke, and Spencer Hayden. New York: McGraw-Hill.
Mikalovich, M. E. 1990. "Total Quality Management for Public Sector Improvement." *Public Productivity and Management Review.* 14, no. 1.
Pucik, V. 1988. "Strategic Alliances, Organizational Learning, and Competitive Advantage: The HRM Advantage." *Human Resource Management,* 27, no. 1 (spring).

Rist, R. C. 1985. "Social Science Analysis and Congressional Uses: The Case of the United States General Accounting Office." In *Social Science Research and Government: Comparative Essays in Britain and the United States,* ed. M. Bulmer. Cambridge, England: Cambridge University Press.

———. 1992. "Program Evaluation in the United States General Accounting Office: Reflections on Question Formulation and Utilization." In *Advancing Public Policy Evaluation: Learning From International Experiences,* ed. J. Mayne, M. L. Bemelmans-Videc, J. Hudson, and R. Conner. Amsterdam: Elsevier Scientific Publishers.

Schon, D. A. 1985. "Organizational Learning." In *Beyond Method: Strategies for Social Research,* ed. Gareth Morgan. Beverly Hills: Sage Publications.

U. S. General Accounting Office. 1990. General Government Division. *Office of Personnel Management: Better Performance Information Needed.* Washington, DC: U.S. GAO.

5

Formative Evaluation and Organizational Learning: The Case of the Belgium Postal System

Philippe Spaey and Fabienne Leloup

Up until the beginning of the 1970s, the Belgian Postal Service was considered throughout the world as a model of an efficient public organization. In the last twenty years, however, primarily due to the economic recession, the situation and the image of the postal service have deteriorated considerably. More specifically, the main characteristics of this deterioration of postal services in Belgium include budget cutbacks, reduced staff, lack of training for new staff, stagnation of salaries compared with the private sector, demoralized personnel feeling increasingly insecure, increased complaints from users, deteriorating status of civil servants, and a tarnished image with public opinion. It is a clear example of what is being termed in many countries *hollow government.*

Numerous studies and polls published in the 1980s show that the citizens of Western countries want to see a marked improvement in the quality of services offered by public organizations. But before such an improvement in the public services can be attained, their present condition must first of all be evaluated in relation to the resources, constraints, and objectives of the organizational system. Secondly, policymakers and the public services themselves will need to proactively use the results of such evaluations to adapt their objectives, allocation of resources, and procedures accordingly.

This is the context in which the Belgian Postal Service was restructured between 1985 and 1991 along the lines of a study recommended by the consulting firm Team Consult in 1985. In addition, the postal service was recently transformed into an independent public company (law of 21 March 1991). For its part, our evaluation study has sought to develop a preliminary assessment of these efforts at organizational improvement.

The purpose of this chapter is first to specify the origin and contents of our research and then to present the main results and reactions they elicited within the postal service itself. Finally, we wish to address the issue of whether our evaluation has contributed to changes and organizational learning in the postal service.

Origin and Contents of the Research Study

The starting point of our evaluation was a report entitled "La Nouvelle Poste" ("The New Postal Service"). This report proposed an action program and was prepared by an outside consultant on behalf of the postal service. Copies of the report and its recommendations were distributed to the 45,000 members of staff in 1989.[1]

The main thrust of this action program consisted of four key points as follows:

1. The postal service has two new tasks to fulfill. Its first aim should be to satisfy all its customers by giving them quality service that meets their needs. The second aim should be to ensure that it becomes a modern enterprise, both profitable and concerned for the public interest.
2. These new tasks will be impossible to accomplish without a renewed structure and a new status. This structure should be autonomous, flexible, and adaptable. It should also assume the renewal of material resources (buildings, means of transport, equipment) and human resources.
3. The postal service should take up the challenge of competition because its performance will improve (fewer state subsidies and reduced staff, higher operating income, slightly higher rates).
4. The renewal of the postal service should involve the creation of a different corporate climate: the introduction of efficient management tools, more frequent consultation with the staff over decisions affecting them, and keeping them better informed. The staff should have more interesting jobs due to their increased share of responsibility at all levels, vocational training (techniques, marketing, management), and

new career opportunities based on professional skills and adequate remuneration.

We began by distributing the "Nouvelle Poste" report to all staff and users and conducting an evaluation study of a post office in the area of Mons. We wanted to carry out a "formative evaluation" as defined by specialists on the subject. According to Rist (1989–90: 82), "formative evaluation focuses on identifying and understanding the internal dynamics of programs as they actually operate." For its part, the Evaluation Research Society (1982: 9) defines this type of analysis as "testing or appraising the processes of an ongoing program in order to make modifications and improvements. Activities may include analysis of management strategies and of interactions among persons involved in the program, personnel appraisal, surveys of attitudes toward the program, and observation." Monnier (1987: 113) speaks about "endoformative evaluation," the purpose of which is "to inform the protagonists of the program so that they can modify their conduct, improve the action and thereby transform the aim itself."

In the case under review, the formative (or endoformative) evaluation has a triple objective, namely to:

1. Assess, through a sample survey of four categories of actors (i.e., users, postal service staff, managing civil servants, and political decision makers) within the postal service system, what are the general perceptions of these different actors with respect to (a) how this organization functions and (b) the changes ushered in by the action program known as "La Nouvelle Poste."
2. Identify the main changes and improvements that postal service staff, users, and the managers of the postal service wish to see introduced.
3. Assess whether our evaluation study contributed to the acquisition of organizational learning inside the postal service.

To conduct our study, we chose the main post office in the town of Ath (25,000 inhabitants, in the province of Hainaut). This is a medium-sized post office, which, nonetheless, carries out numerous different operations: sorting for a region of 100,000 inhabitants, accounting, serving customers, routing national and international mail, and delivering in the surrounding region.

To meet the criteria of a "formative evaluation," we interviewed postal service staff and users. The study on the users has not been finished and will not be included in this chapter. Conversely, the survey of postal service Staff is the pivotal point of our analysis. We have asked managerial civil servants (at the regional and national level) and political decision makers for their reactions to the results of this survey.

Of the sixty employees of the main post office in the town of Ath, we interviewed twenty-five who comprised the following:

- the principal collector, head of the Post Office (in frequent contact with the customers and all the staff);
- six counter clerks (in daily contact with the customers);
- seven postmen (of whom five distribute the post daily to the customers); and
- eleven employees having no contact with the customers.

Altogether, twelve out of twenty-five employees have daily or frequent contact with users of the post office and other postal services. The reception from the staff was positive. But some expressed skepticism with regard to any use of the results of the evaluation by the postal service. The interviews were conducted in February 1991.

The interview guide is divided into five parts: organization, customers, buildings and security, corporate culture, and future prospects. These parts correspond to the present characteristics of the postal service and to current and future changes that are to be made within the framework of "La Nouvelle Poste" and "La Poste, Entreprise Publique Autonome" ("The Postal Service as an Independent Public Company").

The Postal Service as an Independent Public Company

During the preparation, implementation, and assessment phases of the inquiry, the Belgian government and Parliament drafted, debated, and enacted the "Law of 21 March 1991 on the reform of certain economic public companies."[2] This law is a decisive step in the overhaul process of the postal service as it enables this service to become a public company with wide managerial independence, in particular as regards human resources, the development of new revenue generating activities, and the setting of rates (Nuchelmans and Pagano 1991).

The law of 21 March 1991 commits the postal service to a process of change that will modify radically its operating conditions by: introducing profitability and productivity criteria, rendering state controls more flexible and assigning greater responsibility to managerial bodies, internationalizing competition, taking the interests of users into account, and consulting and motivating the staff. Nevertheless, we came across a paradoxical observation during our survey when the Parliament was debating the bill and the press was publishing regular articles on the topic. During the interviews, we observed that most members of the postal staff had a very vague notion of the bill and of its implications. Few of the staff had specific information on the proposed changes. And even fewer staff had grasped the important implications for their own work. The debates at the top were not filtering down into the postal system itself. Among those few staff who were knowledgeable about this legislation, they were very skeptical about the proposed changes for their professional life and their company. The implications for organizational learning and change in such a climate are clearly negative.

The Results of the Survey

The results of the interviews have not produced any "revelations" about how the postal service operates nor on the state of morale among the staff who work there. Nevertheless, the survey did prove useful in that it was able to gauge rather thoroughly the perception, opinions, and image of the postal service among its own staff.

Organization

A majority of the staff who were questioned (eighteen of twenty-five) decided to work for the postal service for reasons that were not positive: eight could not find other employment; four needed work; three had no particular reason; two for job security reasons; and one because his father was a postman. These answers can be interpreted in two parts: postal service jobs are not sufficiently attractive, and people who work in them do not seem to be very motivated. Only seven staff members showed personal initiative (entrance examination, sending in a curriculum vitae) with a view to working for the postal service.

Whereas nineteen employees say that the quality of their work is evaluated, sixteen affirm that this evaluation would not bring any change to their work. Thirteen out of twenty-five staff members thought that the quality of their work was not taken into account by the postal service. Such perceptions are not likely to enhance their motivation.

What is yet to be discovered is the impact of such skepticism on their willingness to accept organizational change.

A consultation system between management and elected representatives of the staff (trade unions) does exist at the different levels of the postal service. Nevertheless, the overwhelming majority of employees said that they were not consulted when decisions were taken in the post office (thirteen) or at the regional level (twenty-two), or when possible improvements were made to the running of the post office (seventeen) and their personal work (seventeen). Conversely, nine employees think that they were consulted and that their suggestions achieved results. Finally, most employees believe that their relations with their colleagues (twenty-four), their immediate superiors (twenty-two), and their principal collector (twenty-three) were harmonious.

Although there has been talk about restructuring the postal service since 1985, and such restructuring has been under way since 1989, only eleven out of twenty-five employees can correctly describe the process as it is being implemented. Nine employees have an unfavorable opinion, without being able to say why. Twenty-four employees say they were never consulted. As to the results of this restructuring operation, a large number of employees believe that it will not improve their working conditions (sixteen), nor the service to customers (eleven), nor security in the post office (ten).

The main *motives of satisfaction* mentioned by the employees were as follows:

- in their work—perform their duties properly (six), good relations with other employees (five), satisfying the customer (four);
- in the way the post office is run—good relations among employees (eleven), satisfying the customer (three), no reply (six);
- at the level of the postal service—job security (two), no motive of satisfaction (two), and no reply (sixteen).

The main *motives for dissatisfaction* mentioned by the staff were as follows:

- in their work—lack of material, human and organizational means and resources (sixteen);
- in the way the post office is run—lack of material, human and organizational means and resources (fourteen), no reply (six);

- at the level of the postal service: lack of decision-making power (ten), insufficient salaries (four), no reply (five).

The principal *changes* the staff want to see are:

- the organization (autonomy, participation in decision making, working hours, and salaries) (ten) and material conditions (nine);
- in the way the post office is run—improve the organization (eleven), improve material conditions (six), no reply (seven);
- at the level of the postal service—improve the organization (sixteen), and no reply (seven).

The Customers

Customers often complain about the quality of the reception and service in post offices. Asked about this, the staff reacted in the following manner: some said that the quality of reception depends on the character of the staff (seven); and others said that the complaints are justified (five). These staff would see customer complaints as a problem of the organization. Others believe the faults are divided (five); while 20 percent believe problems with quality service are the fault of the customers (five).

Most staff members (twenty-two) believe that the reception extended to the customers must be improved; but twenty staff members say they have received no relevant training on how to receive customers. How can the quality of the services offered to the customers be improved? Ten employees think that the organization, material conditions, and staff training must all be reviewed while seven staff members gave no reply, and five others said no improvement was necessary.

Corporate Culture

Each staff member under contract of employment undergoes a general introductory training upon taking up his or her duties. Thirteen staff members said that this training has enabled them to do their work better, but twelve others said they had received no training. Most employees said they regularly receive information on the objectives of the postal service (eighteen), the restructuring of the postal service (fifteen), and the development of their own work (twelve). Alternatively, respondents have the impression of being consulted when decisions are taken, be it in their post office (eight) or at the regional level (two).

Eighteen staff members believe that their problems and interests are not well represented in the general management of the postal service. Of interest here is the evident disconnection between the perceptions of the postal staff and the formal organization system. There is an established consultation process in the postal system that is supposed to ensure that staff concerns are represented and heard. Staff reactions suggest this is not the case in practice.

Future Prospects

On 21 March 1991, nearly one month after the interviews, the law authorizing the postal service to become an independent public company was enacted. The media had talked about this change repeatedly in the weeks that preceded the survey. Whereas eight employees said they were informed about this pending change in the postal service's articles of association, seventeen said they were not. Another twelve staff members did not know what this change would entail. Finally, half or fewer of the employees believe that this statute change will have positive effects for the image of the postal service among the public (thirteen), for the postal service itself (twelve), for the customers (eight), and for themselves (eight).

To the question "How do you see your future prospects with the Postal Service?" the majority of staff members (fourteen) gave a reply hardly in keeping pace with the dynamics of change and the transformation of the postal service into a modern company: "I'll just carry on working quietly until I retire" (seven); "My career is almost over, I am not really bothered" (three); "The Postal Service will become more selective" (three); "I'll not finish my career in the Postal Service" (one).

Ten employees gave a reply that was compatible with the dynamics of change: they want to work their way to the top and have an interesting career, better salary, more motivating work, and they recognize the important emphasis that must be placed on quality (ten).

Some Conclusions

The overall impression from the interviews was that the majority of the staff were discouraged, skeptical, and fatalistic about the post office board and any changes that might be introduced to it. Generally speaking, two contradictions emerged from the answers given by the employees: one at the organizational level of the postal service, the other at the level of the individual daily work of each employee.

The project "La Nouvelle Poste," under way since 1989, is at variance with the daily reality of the postal service as experienced by the staff. This project lay stress on the new twin tasks assigned to the Post Office—satisfying the customers and becoming a modern, dynamic and profitable company. These new tasks would be accomplished thanks to the renewal of management structures and the creation of a different corporate climate emphasizing information, cooperation, participation, and vocational training for the staff. But contrary to this ideal image of the "New Post," the staff work daily in a discouraging climate and a bureaucratic organization that gives them too little information, financial incentives, responsibilities, and training.

The employees feel themselves torn between the expectations of the users who wish to find a modern postal service that is dynamic, caring, and fullfilling the needs of its customers and the insufficient means and resources (material, human and organizational) available to them as employees to respond to these expectations. As the replies to several questions show, a large majority of staff members perceive their initial hiring and future prospects with the postal service as a choice by elimination. Such a choice is not very compatible with the will to change expressed by the political decision makers and the executive civil servants of the postal service. Informed but poorly, insufficiently trained and rarely consulted, most staff members seem to work from day to day in a bureaucratic organization that is perceived to offer no prospects for the future. Many employees only find motives for satisfaction in the harmonious relations between colleagues.

But the quality of these personal relations seems to be more of a compensation for general disillusionment than as a lever for change within the organization. The few extended interviews we were able to conduct with executive civil servants led us to believe that some of them are unaware or underestimate how discouraged and disheartened the staff really are.

Reactions to the Results of the Survey

After analyzing the results of the interviews, we drew up a preliminary report. Numerous copies of this document were distributed to the staff of the post office in Ath, the Regional Management of the Post Office Board (Mons), several executive civil servants of the postal service, the minister responsible for the PTT and members of his staff. We asked all our correspondents to read the report carefully and to grant us a thirty-minute individual interview to express their reactions. These interviews were conducted at the end of October and the beginning of November 1991 and were recorded.

Reactions of Postal Service Staff

Seven individual interviews were held at the Ath Post Office with the head collector and six staff members representative of the different categories of personnel. With the exception of the head collector who found the results at times more pessimistic than he believed was warranted, all those interviewed stated that they agree that the results gave a true picture of their daily experiences at the work place. What did surprise those interviewed was that most members of the staff expressed the same negative opinions and shared many of the same feelings of discouragement and disheartening. We also were told that many employees read the report and discussed it among themselves, laying particular emphasis on how the postal service is run and on the future career opportunities for the staff members.

All those interviewed expressed satisfaction because they felt that for the first time, outside observers took an interest in postal employees, treating them as responsible persons and not as numbers. They appreciated being afforded an opportunity to express their opinion. We find this situation paradoxical given the fact that consultation mechanisms are available at all levels of the postal service for staff members to express their suggestions, claims, and complaints to the management through their elected trade union representatives. The question therefore arises whether or not the current system of consultation functions to the satisfaction of the staff. Apparently, the answer is no. It is, moreover, worth underscoring that only one employee mentioned the consultation system and that no reference was made by the postal employees of the trade union representatives. Only the managers of the postal service did so.

Formative Evaluation and Organizational Learning 117

All those interviewed, albeit with slight subtleties at times, asserted that the results of the survey corresponded not only to their own feelings and experiences, but also to those of all the staff at the post office. Such unanimity should give political decision makers and the national management of the postal service pause for reflection. All the more so, as those interviewed believe that "those who decide" are unaware or underestimate the disheartening, isolation, and discouragement of postal service employees. As one staff person commented, "The decision makers are unaware of the actual situation in the field. They base their decisions on statistics." Both staff and executive civil servants told us that the Ath Post Office is not an atypical post office and that the results of the survey on the whole presumably reflect the situation in a large number of post offices throughout the country.

Initially, many employees stated that the evaluation survey and their reading of the report changed nothing in the way the post office was run. The burden of habit, the feeling of helplessness before the administrative apparatus, and isolation from the decision-making centers are just some of the elements cited by those interviewed to justify this lack of change. As the interviews progressed, however, we noted that they started to mention certain indications of change within the post office. For instance, in most departments, the employees discussed the survey results and whether they should be reported to "high places." They also discussed certain problems related to the running of the post office as well as possible solutions.

Most of the employees, however, expressed the view that any fundamental change must come from the top. As they see it, political decision makers and executive civil servants must clearly become aware of the present situation "in the field" of organizational choke points, low remuneration, training and motivation problems, and the decrepitude of the premises and equipment. Only then, staff believe, will decision makers be sufficiently motivated to take the necessary measures to transform the postal service into a modern company. This reasoning, which we heard time and again, echoes the observation many others have made before us in different organizations: The power of the decision makers is often overestimated, while that of the operatives is usually underestimated (Monnier 1987: 73). The staff saw themselves as the recipients of change, not the instigators of change.

Reactions of Executive Civil Servants

Two executive civil servants of the postal service, one at the regional level and the other at the national level, gave us interviews to express their points of view on the evaluation report. In addition, the report was distributed to seven regional inspectors of the Postal Service, who subsequently told us that the conclusions of the report correspond to the situation they have observed in numerous post offices in their respective region.

For the regional manager of the Ath Post Office, the results of the survey came as no surprise. He believed they reflected the real situation of numerous post offices. He said many postal service officials are well aware of this situation. The new element is that such a diagnosis has been made by independent observers and communicated to the national management of the postal service and to the minister for the PTT. The regional manager found our survey useful in that he believed it might have more influence on political decision makers than would a similar study conducted internally by postal service civil servants. Interestingly, he expressed basic reservations about the entire direction the changes were taking, wondering out loud to us as to whether turning the postal service into an independent public company was appropriate. He questioned whether the postal system could adsorb a radical change in the way it is run, in its activities, its results, and the basic motivations of the staff.

The national manager we interviewed was the most defensive about the present and most optimistic about the future. He was taken aback by how negative the replies were of those interviewed, the demoralization of the staff, and their skepticism as to prospective changes in the postal service. Again and again he underscored the existence of a consultation system and negotiations with trade unions, and on the plethora of information that is disseminated in the postal service. However, he admitted that the high rate of absenteeism among the postal service staff was an indicator of the problems confronting the postal service when it comes to managing human resources. In the end, he said he understood the current disheartening of postal staff, though not their lack of hope in the future. The national manager also said that the opportunities to turn the postal service into a modern, profitable company are sound, and that the new law on public companies provides ample perquisites to those who wish to forge ahead with the restructuring of the postal service.

Reactions of Political Decision Makers

We sent the report to the minister responsible for the PTT and to several members of his staff. The minister asked one of these staff to comment on the report. The person selected was an executive civil servant in the postal service assigned to the staff of this minister for several years, and consequently someone with an important role in policy decisions concerning the postal service. Furthermore, he is thoroughly familiar with the postal service. He has had a twenty-five-year career with assignments in virtually all the echelons of the hierarchy. He has also been among the political decision makers for a number of years. The reflections and comments of this individual are of importance in gauging the level of commitment to and understanding of the changes underway within the postal system.

His reactions and reflection can be summarized as follows. The survey is very valuable because it is conducted by observers outside the postal service. The final report, in summary form, should be sent to all new members of the postal service. A few reservations notwithstanding, he believed the report to be a true reflection of the situation of the postal service and its staff. With 45,500 employees, the postal service is the largest employer in the country. In terms of revenue (BEF 50 billion or U.S. $1.38 billion), it is among the top thirty Belgian Companies (Poste 1991: 34). But the management of human resources is particularly complex and difficult because the level of training and qualification of most staff members are rather low.[3] Many postal service employees are disheartened because their salaries are low, they are facing difficult working conditions and schedules, and they have rather limited prospects for the future. Thus, in his opinion, the low morale of postal service workers is nothing out of the ordinary; it reflects the overall gloom so characteristic of the Belgian public services since the 1980s.

The senior staff person said the minister for the PTT and the members of his staff do not underestimate the discouragement of the rank and file. Furthermore, he (as the regional manager also noted) was surprised to hear those interviewed say that their concerns and interests were not properly represented. More specifically, he assured that the rate of trade unionism is very high at the postal service and that consultation bodies exist at all levels. The fact that the workers themselves did not believe they were well represented suggests that the minister assumed the organizational structures successfully carried out their functions. In reality, this appears not to have happened. The trade unions were functioning as an oligarchy, not as a representative body. To conclude, he was convinced that the "independent public company" would probably be more efficient and dynamic than the current postal service.

Conclusion: Did Our Evaluation Contribute to Organizational Learning in the Postal Service?

At the end of this brief empirical study, we would like to provide elements for a reply to two interdependent actions that concern the use of results of any evaluation:

1. Did our study contribute to changes in the postal service?
2. Did our study contribute to organizational learning in the postal service?

The postal service was obviously already in the midst of a restructuring process (some of the people interviewed spoke of a "revolution") before we decided to embark on this evaluation. But the fact that executive civil servants of the postal service and members of the staff received us repeatedly and spoke to us openly as outside observers without official authorization was a pleasant surprise. We interpreted this reception and this opening as a positive sign of change. It is worth underscoring, in fact, that for several years now, the postal service has been the focus of repeated criticism from users and the press and has been understandably wary of any initiative that might prove a source of new censure.

The basic transformations under way at the postal service since 1985 and after the enactment of the 1991 law on public companies, can be qualified as "top-down changes." More specifically, politicians and executive civil servants of the postal service, with the help of outside consultants, decided to transform the postal service into a modern, dynamic, and profitable public company. In order for this "revolution" to succeed, the behavior of the staff and the corporate culture must unquestionably undergo radical changes. We agree with Crozier and Friedberg (1977: 30) that change is "a process of collective creation through which the members of a certain organization learn together, i.e. invent and establish new ways of playing the social game of cooperation and conflict and acquire corresponding cognitive, relational and organizational capacities." Consequently, the corporate culture of the postal service and the behavior of the staff cannot be changed alone by decree from on high (Crozier 1989: 71–76). In this regard, Argyris and Schon (1978) make a basic distinction between "espoused theory" and "theory in use." In the case under review, the "espoused theory" in the "Nouvelle Poste" project pertains to profitability, dynamism, efficiency, quality of service to customers, and so forth, while the "theory in use" is that observed in the Ath Post Office—isolation, heavy emphasis on hierarchy, lack of staff participation, no consultation, discouragement, refusal to assume responsibilities, and so on.

Thus, for the current "culture" of the postal service to be changed, the system that produces and reinforces this culture must be changed first. To do so, senior management must first become familiar with and accept themselves this culture and this system. Our data suggest that only when the staff see the changes in the behavior and values of the senior management will they themselves start to believe the change is possible and positive. Stated differently, changes at the bottom will come after changes at the top. At what point will the postal service employees start to change their behavior and culture. Only when they believe that such changes will enable them to create a more satisfactory system for themselves (i.e., more efficient, more open, more diversified, more self-fulfilling, etc.). When these changes take hold at all levels of the organization, the postal system will be going in the right direction to transform itself into a high-performance, high-quality organization.

We believe that our survey made it possible, for the first time perhaps, to describe the main features of the current behaviors and culture of the postal service. Further we believe our data show that the present behaviors and culture constitute a hindrance to the process of change initiated by political decision makers and the Parliament. In this regard, we believe that our study contributes, albeit modestly, to raising the consciousness and facilitating change in the postal service.

However, we detected a disparity between the technical changes that require single-loop organizational learning and the more profound changes that call for double-loop organizational learning. Operations under way for a number of years without much difficulty include the renovation of buildings, the modernization of means of transport, the reduction in the number of sorting centers, the improvement of mail routing methods, and so forth. These are chiefly technical changes that lead to more efficient postal services without unsettling the standards, values, and behaviors inside the postal service.

Conversely, the postal service has set what appears to be a limited objective ("D+1"),[4] which nonetheless it does not manage to achieve[5] because it entails a profound change in behaviors, the organizational system, and the corporate culture inside the postal service. In concrete terms, in order for the "D+1" objective to be achieved fully, the postal service staff at all steps of the process, from the collection, to processing, routing and delivery of mail, must perform their task in consideration of such criteria as efficiency, quality of service offered to customers, punctuality, speed, professional consciousness, and a sense of responsibility. However, such a change is inconceivable without a transformation of the organizational system and the management of human resources inside the postal service. Were such a transformation to occur, we believe we would then be in a position to document a case of double-loop organizational learning.

In a more general manner, it appears that the success of the "Nouvelle Poste" program depends on transforming the postal service into a flexible, dynamic operation keenly concerned about the needs of its customers, and staffed with competent, motivated, and efficient individuals at all levels. Beyond the technical changes and improvements, postal service staff must learn a new culture, new standards, and ways of acquiring new skills. What we are suggesting is that for the postal system to be successful, it must support and encourage double-loop learning for all staff working in all phases of the organization.

By listening to the staff at the Ath Post Office and involving them in the evaluation of the system (and culture) to which they belong, we believe we have rekindled or reawakened a demand for reform, and perhaps even a capability to act at the rank and file level (Crozier 1989: 66; Jobert and Warin 1990: 65–75). The discussions that took place among the staff after the survey and a second series of interviews at the post office illustrate and confirm this observation. The same applies to the demand raised repeatedly by our respondents, namely to forward the results of the survey to the executive civil servants and to political decision makers. Finally, the interviews given by executive civil servants and one political decision maker, as well as the distribution of the final report to all our respondents have increased the flow of pertinent information on the culture and staff perceptions of the postal system. In this context, we could assume that our survey has made a contribution, however modest, to the process of double-loop organizational learning.

Notes

1. This action program was itself the outcome of a study entitled "Postes Belges 90—Plan Directeur Global" carried out by Team Consult in September 1985.
2. See Moniteur Belge (*Official Gazette*) of 27 March 1991.
3. According to the same report, the postal service employs 415 university graduates (or the equivalent), 4,766 graduates of upper secondary education, 10,681 graduates of lower secondary education, and 25,351 holders of primary education diplomas.
4. "D+1" means that a letter posted at 4:00 PM in a letter box in Belgium will be delivered to its addressee the following morning anywhere in the country.
5. As shown by the survey conducted by *Test Achats Magazine* in 1990 (see "L'Efficacité comparée de la poste belge" ["Comparative Efficiency of the Belgian Post"], *Test Achats Magazine* (Brussels), no. 327, November 1990: 8–13).

References

Argyris, C. 1982. *Reasoning, Learning and Action.* San Francisco: Jossey-Bass Publishers.
Argyris, C., and D. Schon. 1978. *Organizational Learning: A Theory of Action Perspectives.* Reading, MA: Addison-Wesley Publishing Co.
Crozier, M. 1989. *L'entreprise à l'écoute.* Paris: InterEditions.
Crozier, M., and E. Friedberg. 1977. *L'acteur et le système.* Paris: Editions du Seuil.
Evaluation Research Society. 1982. *Standards for Evaluation Practice.* San Francisco: Jossey-Bass.
Jobert, B., and P. Warin. 1990. "L'évaluation comme activité de stimulation de l'apprentissage organisationnel." *Evaluation et Décision, Séminaire du Laboratoire Ceops.* Paris: Ecole Nationale des Travaux Publics de l'Etat.
Monnier, E. 1987. *Evaluation de l'action des pouvoirs publics.* Paris: Economica.
Nuchelmans, D., and G. Pagano. 1991. *Les Entreprises Publiques Autonomes.* Bruxelles: Courrier Hebdomadaire du Crisp, no. 1321–22.

Poste. 1991. *Rapport 1990*. Bruxelles.
Rist, R. C. 1989–90. "On the Application of Program Evaluation Designs: Sorting Out Their Use and Abuse." *Knowledge in Society: The International Journal of Knowledge Transfer* 4: 74–96.

6

Effective Internal Evaluation: An Approach to Organizational Learning

Richard C. Sonnichsen

In the introduction to this book organizations are portrayed as reluctant to engage in the difficult challenge of introspection. Basic assumptions underlying organization policies and operations are seldom questioned by responsible managers, resulting in a continuous process of superficially examining problems without arriving at permanent solutions. Limited incentives exist for program managers to critically review their program policies and activities, since the outcomes are generally unpredictable and the potential negative consequences are often perceived to outweigh the problematic positive outcomes.

Those organizations that have attempted to scrutinize their activities and critically examine the underlying assumptions of policies and operations have found it a difficult process, yet evidence exists that when employed it offers significant dividends in improved performance. Government organizations are no exception to this phenomenon. Effective government programs are the stated goal of most public servants, yet attempts to measure, document, and publicize optimal government programs remain elusive. In the United States some inefficiency in communicating program results occurs simply due to the immensity of the federal government effort to discharge the governance process. This condition, however, should not impede the development of effective evaluation procedures designed to measure the performance of government programs.

Notwithstanding the perceived difficulty in critically examining organization programs, the Introduction outlined an organizational learning approach where evaluators, acting as independent, objective observers, funnel information to management, which increases its decision-making capacity. By providing program assessment data, unencumbered by parochial viewpoints of program personnel, evaluators can serve as independent purveyors of program information to officials at various levels in the organization.

Evaluators also assist the organization in the problem-solving process by acting as a link between the program performance level and the management level in the organization. Many times the problems detected in inefficient and/or ineffective programs, during program evaluations, can be traced to the lack of an empirical data base on the program activities. However, the incorporation of information into the decision-making process or knowledge base of an organization is often selective and transient. Many times decision makers "satisfice;" they make decisions without solid empirical data. However, if relevant, useful data are available to decision makers, they may be used and the decision-making process arguably improved. The decision-making model is the dominant model for evaluators functioning in an internal mode (Love 1983b; Mathison 1991).

The technique of program evaluation, a methodology for reviewing the management processes and outcomes of programs, is available with only modest outlays of funds and personnel. This analytical tool for program review and analysis has been demonstrated to be effective in critically reviewing programs and suggesting improvements. Although not universally used, this powerful approach to program review can be an effective mechanism to channel performance feedback to managers as well as executive management responsible for agency performance.

The scenario described in the introductory chapter is that although evaluation is but one of many sources of information in organizations, institutionalized evaluation procedures can make strong contributions to organizational learning and hence to positive organizational change. The questions asked were: Are there empirical data available to support this assertion, and, if so, what organizational conditions, structures, and policies contribute to the effective use of evaluation results for organizational learning and improvement?

This chapter will offer examples where evaluation efforts have contributed to both single- and double-loop learning. The evidence presented is based on research conducted in five federal U. S. government internal evaluation offices in Washington, D. C., and my own personal experience in directing management studies and evaluations in an internal evaluation office for ten years.

The premise here is that the proper combination of organizational conditions, evaluation skills, and managerial attitudes can precipitate organizational learning as a routine organizational occurrence. A model will be offered, depicting the necessary components needed by evaluators in order to engage the organization and make positive contributions to the organizational learning process.

Internal Evaluation

Although evaluation by external evaluation contractors and government oversight agencies has waned in the United States in recent years, the need for evaluation has not diminished. This has given rise to the new phenomenon of internal evaluation offices. This recent trend in the evaluation profession, away from external, contracted evaluations, to internal evaluation offices, represents a major transformation in evaluation practice (Love 1983a; House 1986; Patton 1986; Comptroller General 1988). However, despite this trend and the growth of internal evaluation offices there is still a serious knowledge gap about the conduct of internal evaluation (Love 1983a, 1991).

In 1991, the author compared the operations of five internal evaluation offices in the U.S. government (Sonnichsen 1991). The focus of this research was on the performance of federal internal evaluation units in an attempt to answer the question: What strategies, techniques, organization structures and processes, and philosophies of evaluation are the most effective at (1) optimizing the use of evaluation findings, and (2) influencing the agency decision-making process? The objective of this research was to explore the practice of evaluation in five internal evaluation offices in federal agencies in Washington, D.C., to identify those factors that appear to contribute to the effective performance of an internal evaluation staff in influencing the organization. Retrospectively, these data were reviewed from an organizational learning perspective to determine if effective internal evaluation offices could also be characterized as aiding organizations in the learning process.

Internal evaluation differs from external contracted evaluation by definition since it takes place in an organizational context, yet minimal information is available concerning this endeavor (Love 1991; Mathison 1991). Equally neglected has been the management of these internal evaluation offices (St. Pierre 1982, 1983). Nevertheless, some models for internal evaluation offices do exist. Internal evaluation is the centerpiece for Wildavsky's (1979) ideal, self-evaluating organization. Love (1983b) believes internal evaluators have an ongoing organizational responsibility to act in the capacity of a consulting firm, diagnosing and correcting problems. Typically internal evaluation offices focus on improvement of programs, that is, formative evaluation with the organization itself as the primary client (Love 1983b; Mathison 1991). According to Clifford and Sherman (1983) the internal evaluator challenges assumptions and values, creating alternatives in a supporting mode to the organizational decision-making process. Internal evaluators can also become activists for organizational change to enhance organizational performance (Clifford and Sherman 1983). One approach to organizational change, advocacy evaluation (Sonnichsen 1988), moves the evaluator beyond a neutral observer after an evaluation is completed, to an activist position insuring evaluation findings and recommendations are included in organizational policy debates.

This trend of evaluation toward internal evaluation offices raises the fundamental question of evaluator independence. A critical requirement for internal evaluators is to be perceived as objective and independent and viewed by the organization as impartial observers. There is little doubt that an internal evaluation office is affected, to some degree, by the host organization (Kennedy 1983), but there is insufficient evidence to support House (1986, 1988, 1989) who believes that internal evaluators are incapable of conducting impartial evaluations and become tools of the organization administration (Sonnichsen 1987a, 1989). In fact, Attkisson, Brown, and Hargraves (1978) report that to be useful in human service organizations, evaluation must be developed in synchrony with the organization's management style.

One of the major themes in the evaluation literature is that internal evaluation is an applied enterprise, conducted in the social environment of the organization and has to be viewed within the organizational context (Broskowski and Driscoll 1978). Evaluations conducted by internal evaluators usually serve multiple uses and users; therefore, the evaluations must be responsive to managerial and organizational issues and planned and implemented within the broader context of organizational structures and management processes (Broskowski and Driscoll 1978). Internal evaluators must also deal with traditional organizational issues of power, influence, and access to top agency officials (Clifford and Sherman 1983). Since the primary purpose of an internal evaluation office is to review and comment on the management and outcomes of organization programs, significant attention has to be devoted to the management processes of the organization itself.

Carlson (1979) suggests that evaluation offices are more productive and useful when they report directly to the top person in the organization. In 1970, the Urban Institute recommended that the responsibility for evaluation should be placed at a "level appropriate to the decisions it is designed to assist" (Wholey et al, 1970). They suggested that evaluations should be directed by persons not having a stake in the outcome of the evaluations.

Notwithstanding where evaluation offices are located in the organizational structure, a great deal of influence is exerted by the organization over in-house evaluators with the most obvious influence on the determination of what evaluation will be conducted and the client(s) for the evaluation (Kennedy 1983). Kennedy studied in-house evaluators in sixteen school districts, located in fourteen states, and found that evaluator roles were heavily influenced by organizational dynamics. She discovered that for evaluators to maintain their roles they had to adapt to the organization's problem-solving style. Although successful adaptation assured continuing support for the evaluation enterprise, it often resulted in failure to meet the professional standards of the evaluator's role. Essentially the organizational context defined the evaluator's role.

The literature available on internal evaluation is sparse and at this time there appears to be little consensus on successful methodologies for internal evaluations or on successful internal evaluation models.

Research Methodology

The research described in this chapter attempts to identify those organizational, structural, and management processes that appeared to contribute to the effective practice of internal evaluation in organizations. Subsequent analysis of the data has addressed the discussion here on the outcome of organizational learning.

Five internal evaluation offices at the federal level of the U.S. government, representing law enforcement, land management, housing management, food and drug safety, and public health and human services were selected for case studies. Site selection was a purposeful sample designed to produce organizational diversity and represent a variety of types of evaluation practice. Data were collected primarily through document reviews and interviews with evaluators and program managers.

Characteristics of Effective Internal Evaluation Offices

Evaluation is not a rigidly defined process; therefore, it provides significant latitude and flexibility to the head of an evaluation office in adapting to the organization, defining objectives, conducting evaluations, hiring staff, and interacting with superiors, peers, and subordinates. Because of this, the practice of evaluation encountered at each of the five sites varied considerably, yet each fit the broad definition of evaluation as a tool for organizational improvement. Mayne (see chapter 1) found this diversity in the Canadian federal system as did Leeuw and Rozendal in the Netherlands (see chapter 3). Mayne reports that although evaluation was viewed primarily as a tool for improving program delivery, evaluation played different primary roles in different departments.

Although diversity underscored the types of evaluation practiced in the five U.S. organizations, there were common themes observed among the evaluation offices that contributed to the success of their endeavors. At each U.S. site evaluation practice had been designed to be congruent with the administrative decision-making apparatus of the organization and reflected the management style of the head of the evaluation office. Evaluations, especially those conducted by internal evaluators, are usually not vehicles for discovery, but rather tools for reconciliation of disparate data and opinions, which are used to increase the effectiveness and efficiency of programs by furnishing useful information about program performance to decision makers.

Each of the five evaluation offices recognized that organizational justification for their existence was dependent on the production of useful information for use by the organization. They also realized that ponderous, lengthy, methodologically rigorous research projects were not only not wanted or used but could also be detrimental to the survival of the evaluation office. Encountered among the offices was a sense of timeliness, the notion that data had a shelf life and to be useful they needed to be produced and disseminated with a conscious regard for the events surrounding their need or reason for being requested.

Utility had been adopted as a standard by which evaluations were judged in the organizational deliberative process. Through trial and error the evaluation offices studied have interpreted the informational needs of their organizations as understandable, relevant data furnished to the right client, in a useful format and in a timely fashion. The internal evaluators in this sample had discovered and maintained a balance between epistemological considerations and pragmatism. Sophisticated, rigorous evaluation methods may appeal to the researcher and be sufficiently erudite for professional journal publications but if they lack timeliness and relevance they are unlikely to meet the requirements for organizational consumption. Elegant evaluation design does not have to be avoided in internal evaluation settings but proper recognition that its appeal may be more to the evaluator than the decision maker will help maintain methodology in the proper perspective.

Clearly visible during this research was an attunement of the style of evaluation practice with the character, culture, administrative habits, and political realities of the organization. Internal evaluation offices possess some unique characteristics unavailable to external evaluation contractors. Internal evaluators acquire institutional knowledge over time and develop a cultural awareness that only results from continuous observation of the organization from close proximity. Constant exposure of evaluators to the internal workings of an organization presents opportunities to develop a perspective about what contributes to organization success and what hinders progress toward optimum performance. This accretion of knowledge and culture about organizational decision making processes offers internal evaluators a significant advantage over external contracted evaluators. It clearly increases the likelihood that organization learning will occur when evaluations are conducted in-house.

In addition to the cultural awareness and institutional knowledge evaluators acquire, they have the capacity to develop legitimacy in the organization through the continuous display of credibility, independence, and skill when conducting evaluations. Unless evaluators are viewed by the organization as an integral component in the decision-making process, evaluation will be relegated to ad hoc successes and the ability of evaluation to enhance organizational learning will be greatly diminished.

The most receptive organizational cultures for evaluation were observed in agencies that were homogeneous, single-mission organizations with career-oriented employees who had significant identification with and commitment to the organizational goals. Less organizational acceptance of evaluation as a beneficial management tool was observed where the organizational mission was more diverse.

What was not observed among the five evaluation offices was any agreed upon definition of their organizational role or a consensus agreement on the appropriate client in the organization for evaluation information. One evaluation office viewed the program manager as the primary and only client for the evaluation product; another considered the Congress and the Office of Management and Budget (OMB) as part of their client constituency; while a third office viewed the head of the agency as the client for evaluations. In one organization the evaluation client varied and was significantly influenced by the management style of changing political appointees at the assistant secretary level. The evaluation perspective on the proper client covered a considerable range and significantly affected the way evaluation was practiced in the five organizations.

No common philosophical definition of evaluation was encountered among the five offices; two used evaluation as a change-agent mechanism, one evaluation staff functioned as advisers to management performance review teams, while in two others evaluators built and manipulated large data bases to retrieve program information for individual program managers.

Evidence of the importance of senior management support was evident at all five sites. The interest of the top agency official in evaluation significantly impacted not only the style of evaluation, but also the resources allocated to this function. Without the interest of top agency officials, however, there was ample latitude for the heads of the evaluation offices to tailor evaluations to their own management style.

Organizational Learning Examples

Did organizational learning occur in these offices? The answer is yes; both single- and double-loop examples were encountered. Where there was a congruence of favorable organization conditions and an evaluation staff with clearly defined objectives and established evaluation procedures, organizations were observed to convert evaluation results into learning experiences with demonstrable positive changes in the organization.

A significant example of double-loop learning occurred in the Federal Bureau of Investigation (FBI) in 1975 when the basic philosophical approach to criminal investigations was questioned. Prior to 1975, FBI policy mandated the investigation of all criminal violations of federal law. Performance monitoring of field office investigative activities focused on the production of statistical accomplishments with little regard for the complexity of a case or the impact of the investigation. Encouraged by the FBI Director to review the FBI's investigative approach and seek alternatives, the evaluation office gathered empirical data showing that a de-emphasis on statistical accomplishments and encouragement to initiate complex investigations resulted in more high quality cases with greater impact than under the traditional approach. The evaluation underscored that with finite investigative resources and an infinite number of criminal activities, greater impact could be demonstrated by redirecting investigative resources toward major criminal enterprises (Sonnichsen 1987b).

Persuaded by these evaluation data, the Director, in 1975, mandated that all FBI offices convert to the quality case concept. This FBI example is an excellent illustration of double-loop learning where an evaluation staff assisted an organization in examining the basic assumptions supporting the primary mission of the organization resulting in a positive change and a fundamental reorientation of the priorities and energies of the entire organization.

The inspector general (IG) at the Department of Health and Human Services regularly scrutinizes public health policies and offers alternative approaches to the administration of these expensive programs. The IG evaluation office annually claims millions of dollars saved as the result of their program reviews (Mangano 1990).

One IG study examined conflicts of interest when physicians refer patients to clinics or laboratories that are owned by those physicians. The study found that 12 percent of the physicians in the Medicare program have financial interests in outside health care entities and the patients of these physicians received 45 percent more laboratory services than the Medicare population in general. It was estimated that the higher use of services by patients of physicians owning clinical laboratories cost the Medicare program $28 million in 1987. The evaluation report was furnished to Congress with six options relating to physician ownership and self-referral, and both the IG and the deputy IG for Evaluation and Inspections testified. A bill was passed restricting Medicare payments to physician-owned laboratories. This evaluation uncovered a fundamental flaw in the Medicare reimbursement process and is an example of evaluation contributing to single-loop learning.

The Bureau of Land Management (BLM) uses evaluation as a tool to evaluate performance and can cite both administrative improvements in operations as well as major personnel changes resulting from evaluation activities. General Management Evaluations (GMEs) are routinely conducted in the BLM state offices every four years to assess the administration and management of the office. One of these GMEs uncovered serious management problems with the executive staff in a state and resulted in the removal and reassignment of the state director and five senior managers. Another GME determined that top management of a large administrative center had insufficient management control over the center's goals and initiatives. Based on the GME findings four senior staff at the center were replaced. On these two occasions, the BLM evaluation process demonstrated instances where single-loop learning occurred. These examples demonstrate that evaluators can contribute to both single- and double-loop learning. The effectiveness of the evaluation process appears to vary with the skills of the evaluators, their approach to the evaluation process, and the receptivity of the organization to internal review and self-reflection.

Internal evaluation offices have the potential to contribute to organizational learning by acting as independent observers of the organizational scene, unencumbered by program administration responsibilities, service delivery requirements, and policy development and implementation. Evaluation staffs are essentially liberated from the day-to-

Effective Internal Evaluation 135

day routines that occupy the full-time attention of most managers and executives. Owing no allegiance to particular programs or policies, nor having a stake in the outcomes of organizational operations, evaluators are free to critically examine and question institutional policies and procedures with the only goal being that of organizational improvement. If evaluation staffs are also positioned at the highest level of the organization, the evaluators are insulated from much of the political dynamics of organization business and can offer unbiased opinions on organization operations without fear of recrimination.

Internal Evaluation Model

The varying evidence of evaluation utilization from the five evaluation sites suggests the potential for a model of an effective internal evaluation office contributing to the successful use of evaluation data by the organization. This model contains both process and outcome components allowing it to be utilized either to design an internal evaluation office or analyze the performance of an existing office.

Attributing causality to any single- variable in the constellation of factors affecting the acceptance, use, and impact of evaluation in internal organizational settings is a tenuous enterprise. No single- condition or element was observed to dominate in determining the success of any of the internal evaluation offices. However, a plausible inference was suggested by observing in the aggregate the factors present in those internal evaluation offices where evaluation results were used and had an influence on the organization.

The following conditions and factors were identified as common patterns associated with the effectiveness of the evaluation offices in achieving the goal of influencing the organization through evaluation and contributing to organization learning.

Organizational Conditions:

- The organization has committed sufficient staff and resources to the evaluation office.
- The evaluation office operates as an independent entity.
- The evaluation office reports to a senior organization official.
- Agreement has been established between the management of the evaluation office and senior organization management on the goals and policies for the evaluation office.
- The head of the evaluation office has sufficient rank in the organization

to be recognized as part of executive management.
- Evaluators are organizationally experienced, career employees.
- Evaluators are accepted in the organization as credible, independent, and objective.

Process Factors:

- The evaluation office has defined its role and publicly announced its evaluation agenda.
- The evaluation office self-initiates evaluations.
- The results of evaluations are incorporated in written reports and widely disseminated within the organization.
- Recommendations are issued when evaluations are completed.
- A follow-up procedure is put in place to monitor the implementation status of recommendations.
- The evaluation staff plays an advocacy role in publicizing the evaluation findings and recommendations.

By aggregating the organizational conditions and process factors a model of an effective internal evaluation office can be developed. The foundation for the acceptance and use of evaluation in internal settings was first, the organizational interest and tolerance for scrutiny of activities, and second, the establishment of a visible evaluation protocol. The importance of the administrative aspect of evaluation in institutionalizing evaluation was underscored in the introductory chapter. Lacking direction and/or interference from senior agency officials, the third major factor was the management style and skills of the head of the evaluation office. Effective performance and successful use of evaluation results were most noticeable in those evaluation offices that operated independently, in a receptive organizational environment, with a visible evaluation protocol and a change-agent mentality among the evaluators. Mayne (see chapter 1) examined the organizational and process factors affecting evaluation utilization in the Canadian federal systems with similar results.

In those organizations where effective evaluation characteristics were present, there were examples of double-loop learning. This is not surprising since successful double-loop learning (as discussed in the Introduction) requires a deliberate commitment by the organization to self-examination and the ability to process and act on evaluation results. A case can be made that for organizations to experience double-loop learning, an engagement between the senior management and the

Effective Internal Evaluation 137

evaluators must take place with the expectation that evaluation findings have a value in organizational improvement.

Proper organizational conditions and appropriate process factors can combine to produce an effective internal evaluation office. Its effectiveness can then be measured by observing the following performance criteria:

- The evaluation staff accomplishes its own goals.
- Evaluation is a routine organizational function and accepted by organizational actors.
- The evaluation office receives requests for evaluations from top organization officials.
- The evaluation office receives requests for evaluations from program managers.
- Evaluation results are used in decision-making forums.
- Evidence is available to demonstrate the positive influence of evaluation results on agency programs, policies, and issues.

Reviewing these evaluation outcomes portrays the performance of an internal office and may suggest potential areas for improvement.

Evaluation, when functioning optimally in an organization, furnishes information to the host organization, which is then used for improved performance. This interchange of information creates a symbiotic relationship where the organization supports the evaluation office and benefits from the data produced, while the evaluation function is sustained by creating an organizational dependency on objective, independent information.

Evaluators need to recognize, however, that evaluation is not the sole source of information available to organizations. Organizations have multiple avenues for obtaining information and evaluation is but one source of input. Nor should evaluators believe they are the surrogate learning arm of the organization. Organizational learning is a collective effort involving multiple constituencies. Evaluators, oriented toward active participation in the organization decision-making process can, however, significantly influence the organization and assist in the organization learning process. These findings in the U.S. government are consistent with the Canadian experience, showing that evaluation can play a significant role in influencing an organization if evaluation is adapted to the organizational culture and the evaluators recognize their role as producers of credible information in a timely manner (see chapter 1).

Conclusion

Clearly the internal evaluation offices in this sample each practiced a unique style of evaluation. Evaluation functioned as a management tool of program assessment, defined, practiced, and influenced by its environment. It was observed to be idiosyncratic to the management style of the leader of the evaluation office, adapted to the organizational culture and traditions, and subjected to periodic redefinition by political appointees. Acutely sensitive to the continuing necessity to justify its existence as a "staff" function in a variety of organizational environments, internal evaluation practitioners developed adaptive mechanisms allowing evaluation to be carried out at various levels of effectiveness depending on the situational conditions existing in the organization.

This research underscored two key elements in the establishment of a successful internal evaluation office: (1) a receptive organizational environment, disposed to an internal review process; and (2) the ability of the evaluation office to define and establish a visible protocol for conducting evaluations in the organization. Evidence was available at all five sites demonstrating the importance of a visible evaluation profile and involvement of organization officials in setting the evaluation agenda. However, if internal evaluation is to influence organizational activities and contribute to organization learning, top management support is a necessary but insufficient ingredient to ensure the success of the internal evaluation office.

For full integration of evaluation to take place in an organization and assist in precipitating organizational learning there must be recognition and acceptance of the use of evaluation as an instrument for organizational improvement. This condition can be approached by establishing a public image of evaluation in the organization through solicitation of topics for evaluation from managers, internal publication of the results of evaluations, and issuing recommendations for program improvement. Using this approach the internal evaluation office gains recognition as part of the organizational administrative apparatus and, over time, integrates itself into the culture of the organization. The failure to establish evaluation as a necessary component in the organizational bureaucratic structure subjects evaluation to the political vagaries of transient organizational administrators and the status of a nonessential organizational appurtenance.

Closely following a receptive organizational environment and a visible evaluation protocol as key features for an internal evaluation office was the importance of the leadership of the head of the evaluation office. The skills and style of the person in charge of the evaluation office was reflected in the performance of all of the offices and in the success of the evaluations.

Internal evaluation in organizations was observed to work and contribute to learning, but its success was neither automatic nor effortless. Organizations seeking to incorporate a double-loop learning process can advance significantly in this direction by staffing and funding an internal evaluation office that reports to top management. Allowing it to function independent of programs increases its potential to furnish unbiased information to major organization decision makers.

Optimal effectiveness occurs when the organization believes in the value of evaluation and the evaluation office has recognized and adapted to the culture and decision-making machinery of the organization. Evaluation, successfully practiced in organizations by permanently assigned evaluators is an internally visible enterprise understood by all employees, with the support and agreement of top management on the goals and objectives for the office.

This research has shown that the contribution of internal evaluation to organization learning is greatly facilitated where the organization exhibits a disposition toward critical self-examination. An organization with a history of utilizing the results of inspections, audits, program reviews, or evaluations in its deliberative process has made significant strides toward becoming a learning organization. Evaluators can contribute to the organization learning process, but the receptiveness of the organization to self-reflection is crucial before organizations begin to learn.

Internal evaluation offices, staffed with competent evaluators and established as independent entities can question organizational norms and traditions and produce dramatic changes if there is congruence between organization senior management and the evaluation office on the purpose and goals of the office. It appears that optimal effectiveness results from an organization that welcomes a critical review of its activities coupled with an evaluation office that functions with a visible evaluation protocol, a change-agent mentality, and a recognition and sensitivity to the structure, culture, and administrative apparatus of the host organization. Evaluation does not appear to have a sustained major influence on organizational activities when these factors are absent. The composite model of internal evaluation resulting from this research represents one approach to internal evaluation practice that has proven successful.

References

Attkisson, C. C., T. R. Brown, and W. A. Hargraves. 1978. "Roles and Functions of Evaluation in Human Service Programs." In *Evaluation of Human Services Programs,* ed. C. C. Attkisson, W. A. Hargraves, M.J. Harowitz, and J. E. Soreson, 59–95. New York: Academic Press.

Broskowski, A., and J. Driscoll. 1978. "The organizational Context of Program Evaluation." In *Evaluation of Human Services Programs,* ed. C. C. Attkisson, W. A. Hargraves, M. J. Harowitz, and J. E. Soresen, 43–58. New York: Academic Press.

Carlson, W. A. 1979. "The Management of Outcome Evaluation." In *Evaluation Management: A Selection of Readings,* ed. G. R. Giblert and P.J. Conklin. Washington, DC: Federal Executive Institute, U.S. Office of Personnel Management.

Clifford, D. L., and P. Sherman. 1983. "Internal Evaluation: Integrating Program Evaluation and Management." In *Developing Effective Internal Evaluation: New Directions for Program Evaluation,* ed. A. J. Love, 23–45. San Francisco: Jossey-Bass.

Comptroller General of the United States. 1988. *Program Evaluation Issues.* Washington, DC: General Accounting Office.

House, E. 1986. "Internal Evaluation." *Evaluation Practice* no. 7, 1: 63–64.

———. 1988. "Evaluating the FBI: A Response to Sonnichsen." *Evaluation Practice* 9, no. 3: 43–46.

———. 1989. "Response to Richard Sonnichsen." *Evaluation Practice* 10, no. 3: 64–65.

Kennedy, M. M. 1983. "The Role of the In-House Evaluator." *Evaluation Review* 7: 519–41.

Love, A. J. 1983a. "Editor's Notes." In *Developing Effective Internal Evaluation: New Directions for Program Evaluation,* ed. A. J. Love, 1–3. San Francisco: Jossey-Bass.

———. 1983b. "The Organizational Context and the Development of Internal Evaluation." In *Developing Effective Internal Evaluation: New Directions for*

Program Evaluation, ed. A. J. Love, 5–22. San Francisco: Jossey-Bass.
———. 1991. *Internal Evaluation: Building Organizations from Within.* Newbury Park, CA: Sage.
Mangano, M. F. 1990. "Evaluation within the U. S. Department of Health and Human Services, Office of Inspector General." In *Inspectors General: A New Force in Evaluation: New Directions for Program Evaluation,* ed. M. Hendricks, M. F. Mangano, and W. C. Moran, 25–36. San Francisco: Jossey-Bass.
Mathison, S. 1991. "What Do We Know About Internal Evaluation?" *Evaluation and Program Planning* 14, no. 3: 159–65.
Patton, M. Q. 1986. *Qualitative Evaluation Methods.* Beverly Hills: Sage.
St. Pierre, R. G. 1982. "Management of Federally Funded Evaluation Research: Building Evaluation Teams." *Evaluation Review,* 6, no. 1: 94–113.
———. 1983. "Editor's Notes," In *Management and Organization of Program Evaluation: New Directions for Program Evaluation,* ed. R. G. St. Pierre, 1–3. San Francisco: Jossey-Bass.
Sonnichsen, R. C. 1987a. "An Internal Evaluator Responds to Ernest House's Views on Internal Evaluation." *Evaluation Practice* 8: 34–36.
———. 1987b. "Communicating Excellence in the FBI." In *Organizational Excellence: Stimulating Quality and Communicating Value,* ed. J. S. Wholey, 123–41. Lexington, MA: Lexington Books.
———. 1988. "Advocacy Evaluation: A Model for Internal Evaluation Offices." *Evaluation and Program Planning* 11, no. 2: 141–48.
———. 1989. "An Open Letter to Ernest House," *Evaluation Practice* 10, no. 3: 59–63.
———. 1991. "Characteristics of High Impact Internal Evaluation Offices." DPA diss., University of Southern California.
Wholey, J. S., J. W. Scanlon, J. S. Duffy, J. S. Fukumoto, and L. M. Vogt. 1970. *Federal Evaluation Policy: Analyzing the Effects of Public Programs.* Washington, DC: Urban Institute.
Wildavsky, A. 1979. *Speaking Truth to Power: The Art and Craft of Policy Analysis.* Boston: Little, Brown and Company.

PART III

When Do Governments Learn?

7

Facilitating Organizational Learning: Human Resource Management and Program Evaluation

Marie Louise Bemelmans-Videc
Bjarne Eriksen
Edie N. Goldenberg

Does program evaluation contribute to organizational learning? If so, under what circumstances? What are the institutional arrangements that facilitate this learning? As stated in the introductory chapter, institutionalization is a primary condition for utilizing evaluation information in a systematic way. Shared expectations regarding the need for and utility of evaluations triggers the institutionalization of the evaluation function. Human Resource Management's (HRM) cultural functions, in transmitting values and sanctioning particular behaviors related to the use of evaluations, can enlarge the organization's commitment to the idea of evaluation and confirm its role in the administrative process.

HRM is often systematically integrated into the organization's total strategic management.[1] Therefore, it becomes a part of the expression of the organization's "theories-in-use," that is, the organizational philosophy. When this is the case, HRM becomes an instrument that creates the conditions for single-loop learning. If the organization aims at facilitating double-loop learning, it should strive—through (among others) HRM—to train its members to appreciate information indicative of mismatches between the current organizational philosophy and the actual demands of the organization and its environment. Double-loop learning would presuppose that in its values, the organization stresses its proclivity to change, that it would allow variety and competition between various views (Hedberg 1981). It therefore should not be hindered by the rigidity of administrative (and political) philosophies. For central governments, impulses for change may also come from contacts with universities, research institutions, and people who preach a different sermon, thus inducing government to rethink its political and administrative theories and practices.

The objective of our research is to offer an overview of the role of personnel policies as they relate to the activities of program evaluation in a number of European countries, in the United States and in Canada. From comparisons among the actual degree of institutionalization of the evaluation function, we hope to deduce indications of HRM's potential as a facilitator of organizational learning. To avoid any misunderstanding, we stress that we look at the role of HRM as a facilitator, creating necessary (though not sufficient) conditions for organizational learning through evaluation.

Our research is of a comparative nature: "There is no reason to believe there exists an easy and straight-forward entry into comparative social research. All the eternal and unsolved problems inherent in sociological research are unfolded when engaging in cross-national studies" (Oyen 1990: 1). Our special problems are the availability of data and, naturally, the degree of their comparability. Even more challenging is the question of the actual meaning of concepts like evaluation in different cultural contexts (Ferrari in Oyen 1990: 77).

Learning from Evaluation:
The Nature of Administrative Judgment

Evaluatory evidence can provide information to improve political and administrative judgment—to make better informed decisions. Let us take a closer look at the art of judgment (Vickers 1965), which is essential to the activity of administering. The way in which an official approaches an issue will depend on his or her values. Values may be defined as "concepts of the desirable with motivating force" (Hodgkinson 1982: 120) and these concepts may stem from many sources: religious and political convictions as well as from individual, psychological, and social-psychological aims and needs (power, ambitions, emotional and physical needs, etc.). The individual's position in the group or the organization will also be of vital importance: it induces decision behavior that ranges from strategic misrepresentation to the use of information to symbolize a commitment to rational choice (Feldman and March 1981). Last for our purposes, but certainly not the final factor, is the individual's training in a specific discipline as a factor conditioning his/her appreciation of information.

The models associated with the art of program evaluation have their roots in the social and the economic sciences. These (and other) professional disciplines and associated frameworks represent value judgments and have corresponding functions in reality judgments. An official will normally disregard any facts that do not seem relevant to his/her personal, professional, or organizational duties and values.
In separately looking at the personnel policy instrument for conditioning the individual's readiness to appreciate evaluatory information, there is the obvious danger of overlooking the actual role of evaluatory information, for example, the quality of the information itself, power constellations, and ideological waves. Indeed, rational information is but one among many contending factors in the political administrative context.

Since we cannot measure the relative weight of those factors, we look at HRM as a facilitator of learning: specifically in its ability to enlarge the willingness of an organization to incorporate evaluatory information in decision making, thus creating a necessary condition for institutionalization. This will mainly be achieved by influencing the primary rules of the game (cultural components) in such a way that argumentation will favor the use of evaluatory information.

The Socialization and Sanction Functions

Since organizational norms and values are at the heart of organizational learning, we concentrate on the socialization function of HRM, describing (pre- and postentry) recruitment and selection procedures, education, and training. The socialization function is complemented by the sanctioning function, which relates to positive and negative incentives to recruit and use evaluation expertise.

Socialization is understood as the transmittal to the individual of a group's or organization's cultural elements (norms, values, beliefs, goals, etc.). Socialization from a managerial point of view is therefore the process whereby the organization orients the individual toward those values and beliefs that it deems ultimately important in the light of organizational goals. The values that are at stake crystallize themselves as the roles and rules of the organization. A crucial factor in the disposition of administrators to use evaluation information will be the degree of centralization in personnel management and the degree to which a uniform policy may be imposed on the entire administration. As we shall see, in many countries, the degree of centralization in personnel management is decreasing, leaving considerable discretionary room for departments and agencies and individual line managers within these units.

Recruitment and selection criteria and procedures are highly conditioned by the characteristics of the administrative system itself. For example, it is possible to examine the degree of politicization of the civil service and the nature of the career system, whether the system is open as in the United States, or closed, as in France. Likewise, the educational system, in so far as it educates the political and administrative elite, will be influenced by these characteristics. Finally, historic and cultural factors, like the perception of the very nature ("the essence") of government, the administrative ideology, the image of officialdom, and the criteria for proper political and administrative judgment, will all influence the educational paths of the elite (Rohr 1991).

Thus, political science and public administration are perceived to have high relevance in the United States for public service, reflected in the existence of schools of public policy on a considerable scale. This is to be contrasted with their low salience in Britain where there seem to be no equivalents (Bulmer 1987: 35). National cultural and political characteristics will also influence preferences as to particular kinds of training for both political and civil service positions, for example, "generalists" (associated with a legal training in France and Germany or a training in the humanities in Great Britain) versus "specialists," again with different professional associations, academic disciplines, or functional domains. Educational requirements are therefore indicative of the relative appreciation of a training in the policy sciences or related subjects.

What are the characteristic modes of thinking of the professions represented in the relevant echelons of the administrative apparatus?

Do they resemble in any fashion the models and methods of policy analysis and evaluation? In other words: how much trouble would it take to convince officials of the analytical and instrumental (strategic) value of policy evaluation? Research indicates that educational background does make a difference for the utilization of evaluatory research (Leviton and Hughes 1981: 540).[2]

In-service training and development figure prominently in modern philosophies of "management of human resources," organizational goals once again forming the ultimate point of reference. Apart from experience and coaching by superiors, personnel development takes place via training programs. These programs show, to an increasing degree, management development components. The very concept of "public management" has explicitly underlined the frame of reference for the policy (and/or administrative) process, and introduced more concretely than before the associated concepts of planning, implementation, and, indeed, evaluation of policies and programs.

The sanctioning and control function should be considered in close connection with the socialization function, since the one complements the other. We have concentrated here on personnel policies with regard to remuneration and career policies and the organizational placement of the evaluation function. What may be deduced from remuneration and career policies regarding the appreciation of policy analytical skills? For instance, is the organizational practice one of job staffing or career staffing? Are specialist skills the dominant criterion, or are career and remuneration policies structured so that specialists are gradually prepared (via rotation) for managerial positions in which their professional skills play a less prominent role? In this case, evaluation expertise may become part of more general managerial skills implying a gradual introduction of evaluation as part of the necessary managerial tools. This approach should be reflected in the subject matter of management oriented training courses.

Two Waves in the Institutionalization of the Evaluation Function

In the next section, we shall present the profiles of the United States, Canada, and a number of European states.[3] In the sequence of presentation, we shall follow the "two waves" in which central governments introduced the evaluation function. The "first wave" countries, introducing evaluation as early as the 1960s, are the United

States, Canada, Sweden, and Germany. In the "second wave," starting by the end of the 1970s and still continuing, are the other countries offering convincing examples of institutionalization: Norway, Denmark, the Netherlands, Great Britain, and only recently Finland and France (Derlien 1990a).

The different waves are explained by general social developments, both political and economic, and by constitutional differences. As for the latter, the very idea of control underlying evaluation has been worked out differently in the relation between the legislative and the executive (Mény 1990: 288). The specific nature of institutionalization was further linked to the intended uses of evaluation. For the first wave countries, the link was between evaluation efforts and interventionist programs while for the second, the link was between cutback management and budgetary review procedures. On the supply side there were developments in the basic sciences providing policy evaluation with a professional methodology. The professionalization process is under way at different speeds in the various states. Countries taking the lead in professionalizing the art have also been leaders in adopting evaluation as an instrument of public management (Bemelmans-Videc 1992).

Evidence from Ten Nations

The United States of America

The United States has had an innovative role in both the development of the relevant theory and methodology of evaluation and in its actual introduction in administrative practice (Rist 1990). When we look at the presocialization mechanisms, this is confirmed by a leading role in providing professional, academic training in the policy sciences. The policy sciences emanated from the applied social sciences, economics, political science, and public administration (McCurdy 1986: 40–45; Henry 1987: 63–68). Policy training of public officials takes place in the context of university-based graduate programs, usually leading to either a Master's degree in Public Policy (MPP) or Public Administration (MPA) or a Ph.D.

The university public policy schools tend to be relatively new, often established fewer than twenty years ago, and many universities have developed new institutes over just the last few years. They show rapid success. Their programs are quantitatively rather than theoretically oriented, dominated by economics rather than by political science, and aimed at attaining professional rather than disciplinary standing (Jann, in Wagner et al. 1991: 123). Jann offers tentative explanations by locating the development of U.S. public policy training in its political context: the development is influenced by the short-term political climate and by long-term characteristics of the American polity as well as by down-to-earth considerations of academic policies and politics. Even though the policy programs are children of the "reform period," they are doing exceptionally well under the changed circumstances of today. The dominance of quantitative methods and economics, and, since the 1980s, a renewed emphasis on management in the public policy programs are qualified by Jann as a "neoconservative fashion" in the public policy field, which strengthened professional ambitions and is suited to the American structure of government, with its open structure and competing power centers (Jann, in Wagner et al. 1991: 124–25).

A survey of twenty-one of the leading university-based public policy institutions done for this study confirms this picture: schools teach policy analysis and utilize extensive training in quantitative methods. They offer specific courses in program evaluation as part of the curriculum. Although curriculum requirements vary from MPA or MPA-equivalent program to program, there is some tendency in these programs toward an "inner core" of six areas of the field: public administration, research methods, public finance, policy analysis, personnel, and politics, and most master's programs offer five of the six (Cleary 1989). Curriculum standards needed for accreditation of a public administration program by the NASPAA (National Association of Schools of Public Affairs) demand (among others) "a common core component designed to produce professionals capable of managing in the public sector." The three broad areas considered essential are: management of public administration, organizational design and the application of quantitative and qualitative techniques for policy and program formulation, implementation and evaluation, and decision-making ability.

The attractive, practical orientation of the programs, claiming generalist training, has probably furthered the placement of graduates within the federal government. Some provide few recruits for federal government, but instead offer local communities and state governments with newly trained personnel. In addition to training future managers, many professors at the major schools pursue research or act as consultants for government agencies. In addition to the graduate programs, a small number of the institutions offer university-based executive programs, from several days to one or two semesters, for formal training of career civil servants. These programs emphasize less skill building and more management of public policy issues and personnel. These courses have been popular for some time with many executive departments. Policy analysis is woven into the leadership development modules.

When we take a closer look at the selection criteria and the resulting representation of professions in the higher civil service, it becomes clear that the U.S. federal bureaucracy is heavily populated with specialists.

> Over a third of the positions in the Senior Executive Service are occupied by scientists and engineers.... Most of the professionals at these high levels have administrative or supervisory posts; nonetheless, they remain specialists, not generalists, for they typically oversee work restricted to their special fields. American top executives, then, cannot be thought of as a single pool of general administrators, for not only have most of them been educated for specialization but their career progress has been up specialized professional ladders, whether within or outside the government. (Fesler and Kettl 1991: 144).

A 1988 survey of career federal executives found that 70 percent of the executives have graduate degrees, 27 percent have a bachelor's and 3 percent less than a B.A. (Office of Personnel Management 1988a).

Entry into positions in the federal civil service has traditionally been achieved through several means: (1) through assembled written examinations predominant till 1982; (2) under the Office of Personnel Management's authority, agencies develop and use their own selection procedures; or (3) unassembled examination of training and experience.

This latter means occurs when the type of position that is being filled requires specific academic training such as engineering, nursing, psychology, etc. There are also a number of smaller programs focused on specific groups.[4] In 1989 approximately 32 percent of all new hires in the government were hired by agencies from lists provided by the Office of Personnel Management (OPM), which screened the applica-

Facilitating Organizational Learning 153

tions. Approximately 68 percent were hired by individual agencies directly after using agency procedures to screen the applications.

The overall picture of the professional background of both higher civil servants and politicians is one of a strong representation of the natural sciences and technology and of the social sciences. Most strongly represented in the early 1970s among the civil servants and the political executives in the United States were technology and the natural sciences with 42 percent among the higher civil servants and 10 percent among the political executives, the social sciences (29 percent and 38 percent), followed by law (18 percent and 28 percent), and the humanities (6 percent and 7 percent) (Aberbach et al. 1981: 51–53).

Campbell (1983) reported the results of a comparative study of officials working in the departments and agencies responsible for government-wide coordination and control in the United States, the United Kingdom, and Canada. He found that 51 percent of his U.S. respondents had received graduate degrees in social science fields as compared to 27 and 37 for, respectively, the British and Canadian respondents. The bulk of the American officials had done their advanced work in economics or political science.

A number of occupations represent the core from which higher civil servants engaged in policy analysis/evaluation can be drawn: program analyst, management analyst, budget analyst, social science analyst, operations research analyst, economist, and General Accounting Office (GAO) evaluator. Academic training for these occupations can be in any field (with the exception of economists and operations research analysts) with the social and behavioral sciences predominating.

The U.S. civil service can be characterized by diverse training institutions, differing opportunities for career advancement, and a lack of consistent criteria within the personnel decision making process. Many institutions offer notably differing forms of training for future and present civil servants. Training for federal employees is authorized by the Government Employees Training Act of 1958. Under this law departments and agencies are required to establish programs for employee development. Each agency is to provide for the continuing development of its higher level managers and executives. Each individual at the SES level must have an Individual Development Plan (IDP) to ensure maintaining currency in appropriate areas. Most IDP's include Federal Executive Institute training as a component, but do not specify particular skill requirements such as program evaluation training.

The Office of Personnel Management (OPM), upon request, assists agencies in developing and improving their training programs. OPM also offers training that is applicable to all agencies through its network of training and seminar centers: five regional training centers, three executive seminar centers that offer more intensive training for mid-level managers, and a Federal Executive Institute offering a longer residential program for senior mid-managers. Courses focus on generalist senior executive roles and personal leadership assessment and development. Evaluation-related courses offered under the heading of Management Sciences include: Introduction to Program Evaluation, Program Evaluation Methods, Data Collection and Analysis, Management Analysis and Review, and Measuring Efficiency in Government. In addition, policy-related training opportunities are available from a number of private universities.

The United States, leading in the extensive initial development of the planning and evaluation functions within central government, experienced a setback in the 1980s. This retrenchment coincided with the presidency of Ronald Reagan. Evaluation was thought to be a tool of liberal efforts at social experimentation and change. Thus, in his administration, it was viewed as unnecessary and even as in opposition to his philosophy of government. The decline was significant. In 1984, there were approximately 140 government units conducting program evaluations, down from 180 in 1980. Most of the decline occurred within federal departments rather than agencies. The professional evaluation staff in the government nondefense agencies had been reduced from 1507 in 1980 to 1179 in 1984. Eight departments (Agriculture, Energy, Health and Human Services, Housing and Urban Development, Justice, Labor, Transportation, and the Treasury) appear to have centralized their evaluation functions as well as abolished some of the units (Chelimsky 1987; Rist 1990). At present, there is one department (Health and Human Services) where evaluation is housed under an Assistant Secretary for Planning and Evaluation. Other departments generally have an Office for Budget and Program Analysis, or an Office of Planning, Budget and Evaluation under an Assistant Secretary for Administration.

As for remuneration policy in general, and career policy in particular, it is very difficult to determine whether evaluation expertise is specifically rewarded (or whether a lack of expertise is negatively sanctioned). Each agency has its own performance appraisal system established within Office of Personnel Management regulations and guidelines. It may be assumed that evaluation expertise is likely to be an important factor in promotion decisions at places such as the GAO. Additionally, there is clearly considerable hiring across central government of graduates of programs of public policy who are well trained in program evaluation. But it would be speculative at best to conclude that evaluation expertise is an important factor in promotion and salary decisions generally in the federal government.

In summary, the United States has had a leading role in providing professional and academic training in the policy sciences. In an open career system, as is the case with the United States, new specialties are periodically introduced. There is no single pool of general administrators with a dominant position and philosophy (e.g., law or economics) that could hamper double-loop learning. The evaluation-relevant sciences are strongly represented. In postentry training, general managerial as well as evaluation courses are given. The established place for policy analysis and evaluation in pre- and postentry training corresponds with the advanced evaluation system in the United States government. There seems to be a tendency for centralization in the organizational placement of the evaluation function; the staff or line character of these units differ. Likewise with remuneration policies, there is no clear link with evaluation expertise, apart from specialist posts in specialized units like the GAO.

Canada

In Canada, there apparently were no political or administrative ideologies troubling the acceptance of managerial notions involving the introduction of evaluation and policy analysis as the reforms of the last decades indicate (Kingdom 1990: 57). Since 1977, the evaluation function has been formally integrated into governmental reviews and oversight. The activities of the auditor general in the 1960s and 1970s greatly contributed to this state of affairs (Segsworth, in Rist 1990). For an overview of the present state of affairs, see Mayne in this volume.

A recent national inventory by the Canadian Evaluation Society shows that although few institutions of higher learning offer a full range of evaluation courses, evaluation has acquired a place of its own in academic curricula, either as a subject in its own right or in relation with subjects like planning and policy analysis. Courses cover theory, the application of evaluation techniques on specific fields (Evaluation of Health Service, of Social Work, etc.), and the critical analysis of evaluation reports. Among the institutions offering evaluation courses, public administration faculties are strongly represented, next to education and medicine/health sciences. The political sciences, however, are underrepresented. The March 1990 edition of the *Program Evaluation Newsletter* states that "few people in Canada graduate . . . specifically as program evaluators. . . . No single educational stream or, for that matter, no specific on-the-job experience seems to lead naturally to the practice of evaluation; evaluators come from various places, probably as it should be" (1990: 8).

Historically, the main selection criterion for the higher civil service was intelligence, demonstrated through an annual examination. Disciplinary training has not been considered overly important for success. The recruitment system is of two basic types: via the standard university graduate examination, which remains largely a general aptitude test with a supplementary examination for those interested in a foreign service career; or via skill/knowledge-based examinations for a large number of specific positions. As a result, no one discipline is dominant in the higher civil service in Canada, although the social sciences hold a very firm position. For senior executives in the federal public service in general, it became clear that in the 1980s the percentage of law degrees decreased while the percentage of social science degrees increased, especially economics and political science. In 1983 14 percent had a graduate degree in law and 37 percent in the social sciences (Olsen 1980; Campbell 1983).

Data on the formal education of deputy ministers (the top civil servants in the government of Canada) in 1989 again indicate the strong position of the social sciences. About 20 percent have a law degree, about 30 percent a science and engineering degree, and the remaining half have at least one social science degree. Recent data (Bourgault and Dion 1991) show

> the rise of two disciplines, management and economics, and the relative decline of law studies among deputy ministers. The proportion with an education in engineering and the natural sciences has remained stable since 1917 at about 25 percent. The remainder have been educated in

Facilitating Organizational Learning 157

various fields in the arts and humanities. There is also a growing trend to combine more than one field of education. (1991: 15–17)

The authors have the impression that the main "general education" till 1967 for this highest post in the civil service was law, the prime concern being to establish regulations within both government and Canadian society. Since 1967 economics and, increasingly, management have gained precedence as forms of general education, at a time when efficiency and management have become more prominent concerns.

In general, senior public servants receive little in the way of post-entry training outside the public service. There are some exchange programs with universities, other levels of government and the private sector, but such programs involve very few people. The vast majority of formal training takes place in-house. All senior management category personnel are required to take a series of courses at the Center for Management Development. Policy evaluation is not a large component of these courses in a formal sense. The curriculum reflects a "managerial" rather than a "policy" orientation. The Staff Training Program of the Public Service Commission and the Course Calendar of the Canadian Center for Management Development offer, in addition to many managerial courses, courses in cost/benefit analysis, rational problem analysis, and decision making.

Agencies like the Office of the Auditor General offer in-house training to their own employees. The Program Evaluation Branch of the Office of the Comptroller General (OCG)[5] has always been involved in a substantial way in training activities by providing a series of seminars or workshops and information exchange sessions for members of the evaluation community. These events range from orientation workshops for new members of the community to methodological workshops aimed at more experienced members. Departmental training sessions are also provided upon the request of the Director of Program Evaluation, and assistance is given in the Senior Management Orientation Course and the Career Assignment Program sponsored by the Public Service Commission (*Comptroller General of Canada* March 1990).

Being one of the "first wave" countries, the formal establishment of the evaluation function took place rather early. Since 1977, it has been the policy of the government of Canada that all departments and agencies evaluate their programs and use the findings to confirm, improve, or eliminate their programs. Responsibility for evaluation was assigned to the deputy head (the senior public servant) of the various federal organizations and ministries. The Program Evaluation Branch was created in the Office of the Comptroller General to oversee the implementation of the policy and to coordinate the planning of evaluation activities across government.

With minor exceptions, all departments and agencies have an evaluation unit. Across the forty-three major departments, there are typically about 200 evaluations ongoing at any one time and 100 completed per year. The *Program Evaluation Newsletter* (March 1990) notes that 352 people worked as officers in program evaluation in 1990. About 41 percent were in positions in the Administrative and Foreign Service category, about 25 percent were in the Scientific and Professional category (majority in the Economists-Statistician group); and about 23 percent were in the Management category. The group was rather evenly divided over various hierarchical levels.

As for remuneration and career policies, there are no formal sanctions applying to evaluation expertise. The *Program Evaluation Newsletter* (Comptroller General of Canada March 1990: 9) offers information on "Evaluation as a career":

> organizationally speaking, evaluation has been explicitly identified as an official corporate function. Thus, it has a distinct strategic position. This healthy organizational disposition towards evaluation should be very attractive to career evaluators, in principle at least. Unfortunately, sometimes, by design or as a result of inappropriate position classification the head of evaluation reaches his or her hierarchical limit too early and at too low a level. In most departments, the head of evaluation is ranked among the lowest corporate managerial positions. However, as staff outside the executive group, their position is a relatively good one.

Summarizing our findings, we see that program evaluation has acquired a place of its own in academic curricula and has developed a well-established organizational place within central government. Selection mechanisms result in no one discipline dominating in the higher civil service. The social sciences hold a strong position. There is also an increasing prominence of economics and management. Canada has shown an early formal establishment of the evaluation function at a senior level of departmental organizations, as well as in central staff functions with the OCG. Other sanctioning policies, especially remuneration, provide a somewhat more ambiguous picture.

Germany

Although Germany figures among the "first wave" countries, its evaluation efforts still are "a case of unfinished governmental and administrative modernization" (Wollman 1989). The German administrative management style is often depicted as rather conservative, hampered by a traditional structure "plagued by intense departmentalism" (Kingdom 1990: 202). Modern management concepts like "planning" and "evaluation" are supposed to run against the German bureaucratic tradition in that they threaten both to infringe the latitude afforded to the administration and to challenge the concept of the bureaucracy as simply an administrative machine interpreting and implementing a given legal framework. In explaining the lack of control mechanisms and lack of initiatives to initiate these from the side of the Parliament, Mény (1990: 191) also points out the "extremely strong juridical tradition, which includes juridical controls" making parliamentary monitoring less essential.

Initiatives for an institutionalization of evaluation date back to the end of the 1960s and the early 1970s. Despite widespread demands, institutionalization as part of a general administrative rationalization of executive and legislative practices continued rather in a patchwork fashion. The evaluation culture was little developed (Derlien 1990a). "To attribute this... primarily to the inherent conservatism of the bureaucracy could be an overstatement of its influence in decision making" (Kingdom 1990: 205).

Commentators (Kingdom 1990; Hellstern and Wollman 1989; Wollmann 1989; Derlien 1990b) also point to political and constitutional factors such as:

- compromise and consensus as naturally resulting from a system founded on coalition government;
- the constitutional division of powers leaving rights on many issues to the states, and where the federal level has the right to regulate, implementation and administration has to go through the states;
- the strength of the individual minister (Ressortprinzip); and

- the tradition of strong, autonomous, external, quasi- and para-governmental institutions.

Ironically, the same reasons that earlier had prevented a rapid spread of evaluation accounted for the interest and growth of evaluation in the second half of the 1970s. As new reform legislations were enacted, information needs grew at the federal level. The constitutional situation separating implementation and administration from regulation and policy development created a need at the federal level to gain feedback information from the states. Evaluation became the substitute for proper federal control. Especially in the fields of social and educational affairs, where the constitutional rights are resting with the states, experimental programs ("Modellprogramme") have been used to introduce reforms and test new solutions to problems. The evaluation of those model programs is a necessary prerequisite to inform the legislature.

In general, screening procedures for the selection of higher civil servants are not related to certain functions, because German higher civil servants are expected to act as generalists in their specific government departments and actually move around between divisions and various specialized jurisdictions. Bonn has a system of career-staffing and not job-staffing. (Sections where specialist knowledge is required will prefer candidates answering those requirements). This tradition of preference for generalist qualities seems to have had organizational consequences: "The tendency is to hive off specialist technical functions to semi-autonomous agencies, thus avoiding the clash between specialists and generalists" (Kingdom 1990: 194–95). This apparently also applies to the policy evaluation function where (semi-)governmental research institutes dominate the field.

Admission exams are not standard procedure except in the foreign Office, where formalized, competitive entry exams are held (as is the case in most other countries). In all the other departments, people are selected in a nonformal way, basically relying on educational certificates, professional expertise, and personal presentation.

In reflection of the legalistic image of the civil service, the monopoly of jurists has gradually declined but still represents 60 percent of the higher civil servants. Economists have increased their numbers to 15 percent (Derlien 1989b). For the social sciences, data are not available. The reduction of jurists has taken place since the middle of the 1960s, basically due to the advent of Keynesian macroeconomic policy.

The German civil service used to be characterized as typical for a closed system. However, there is a decline of traditional uninterrupted internal civil service careers (to 28 percent of the top bureaucrats of the postwar generation) (Derlien 1989a and b). There still is a close association between training in law and uninterrupted civil service careers in the administrative elite. Economists among the administrative elite more often have a mixed career than jurists. With this representation of academic disciplines, it remains difficult to estimate in how far there is an actual acquaintance with policy analysis. Economists will be familiar with cost-benefit analysis but beyond this no social science is to be expected. Some evaluation-related in-service training is offered by the Speyer Academy of Administrative Sciences as well as by the federal in-house training center, the Federal Academy of Public Administration.

Training is not a prerequisite for career progression and there is also no explicit link between evaluation expertise and promotion. Promotion depends on the quality of work done, no matter the contents. There are no career plans, nor does knowledge and experience in specific fields (as, for instance, evaluation) enter the formal appraisal schemes.

What is the organizational position granted to the policy evaluator? One may conclude that only a few centralized offices for evaluations are found at the departmental level, and that coherent and coordinated evaluations are rare even in those ministries with some central steering unit. Quite common is the conduct of evaluations either by special commissions and boards or by governmental or government-sponsored research organizations. Evaluation has grown particularly extensive in the numerous "quasi-autonomous" federal research institutions. In addition, some autonomous government bodies like the Bundesanstalt fuer Arbeit (Government Agency for Employment) have research institutes of their own. It is in those institutions that evaluation flourishes most.

Across the federal government, there is considerable variation in resources, staffing, evaluation quality, and actual interest (Hellstern and Wollmann 1989). Few ministries have institutionalized evaluation activities. Even those that have done so have chosen different organizational strategies for institutionalization, ranging from central planning and delegation of evaluation to outside agencies to an integration in the routine administration. In the Ministry of Telecommunication, the Defense Ministry, and the Ministry of Transportation (Public Rail), inspection units play a major role conducting efficiency studies (*Wirtschaftlichkeitsstudien*). In those ministries with a model or demonstration program, evaluation is often part of the model guidelines. Those ministries involved in law-making have institutionalized some formal procedure (*Prueffragen, Reformvorhaben, Rechtstatsachenforschung*) to rationalize the legislative process. In most ministries, even if they manage large subsidy programs, the more general approach is an ad hoc planning and quite idiosyncratic use of evaluation by the special policy operating unit (*Fachreferat*). Evaluation activities basically take place in the smallest subunit of government departments, in sections where they are often disguised as research activities. Only in the specialized units of a small number of ministries is the evaluation function more prominent (Derlien 1990b: 39–40).

To summarize the evaluation climate, government officials in both the executive and legislative branches are presently more inclined to acknowledge the value of evaluation studies. Knowledge about evaluation techniques and potentials is more extensive among the administration than ten years ago. An attitudinal survey among top civil servants in Bonn (1987) revealed that 51 percent regard evaluation as very useful and another 30 percent as useful (Derlien, CESII-project, no date). At the same time, the links with contract researchers and universities have lead to a fruitful cross-fertilization of contractual evaluation research and policy interests.

Germany has shown an early, but somewhat reluctant effort at evaluation that can be explained by political and constitutional factors and by a legalistic administrative culture. HRM policies reflect this state of affairs. The present impetus for change has induced in-house training programs to compensate for the lack of policy science knowledge. In line with the generalist notion of administrative judgment, we see a tendency to separate out the specialist and technical functions. Thus, the evaluation function has found its main place outside the executive in smaller and more specialized quasi-governmental units.

The Netherlands

With a longer history in *ex ante* evaluation, the Netherlands only institutionalized *ex post* evaluation in the late 1970s and early 1980s. By now the evaluation function is becoming well established within central government as is indicated by a recent (1990) government-wide inventory by the Netherlands Court of Audit (see chapter 3). The most prominent example of an institutionalized evaluation procedure of an interdepartmental and systematic character is the Procedure of Reconsideration (or Review Procedure), which was started in 1981. The procedure is organized in annual rounds and linked to the budget cycle. It touches all policy-fields and has produced more than 100 studies so far (Bemelmans-Videc 1990).

Academic curricula have created a place for the policy sciences since the 1970s. Having their roots in political science and economics, the policy sciences were originally taught in that framework only. In the mid-1970s, policy analysis and evaluation began to be represented in the curricula of the academic programs in public administration. Since these programs started to attract large numbers of students in the early 1980s (especially after separate graduate programs in public administration were being offered), the number of graduates with training in the subjects has increased. Relevant training from a methodological point of view was and is offered in social science programs (especially in sociology), and in economics (cost-benefit/cost-effectiveness analysis). Policy research has shown a correspondingly strong development since the mid-1970s (Leeuw and Boer 1989).

Socialization tools do not indicate the existence of a dominant administrative ideology. In other words, a single tradition does not play a prominent part in recruitment, selection, and career policies. Rather, these policies aim at optimizing the objectivity, legal security, and effectiveness of recruitment and selection. The formal selection criteria are: work experience, educational level, intelligence, social (and if relevant physical) qualities, and so forth. These qualities should be evidenced by the curriculum vitae, diplomas, the results of a psychological test (by the State Psychological Service), references, and interviews. There are no formal entrance exams, apart from the foreign service.

The main characteristics of the existing recruitment and training system are:

- young inexperienced officials are usually recruited for a specialist function and primarily judged as to their qualifications for that position;

- the higher executive positions are mainly staffed via internal promotion and often by candidates from lower, more specialist positions;
- university programs generally provide a specialist education—the number of officials with a more "general" educational profile is still rather limited; and
- postentry development of generalist qualities is often left to individual initiative.

More regular and systematic postentry education and training programs are still rare, although changes may be noticed recently. As we shall see, postdoctoral training programs centering on generalist and managerial qualities are being offered by universities, sometimes in cooperation with government.

As in some other countries, the higher civil service posts are increasingly staffed with academics. Initially they were mainly jurists. But for the last thirty years, the number of economists, sociologists, and other professionals has clearly increased. They have also enlarged their numbers at the higher, generalist levels, gradually replacing jurists and (especially) non-academics. More students in business and public administration are also being recruited. At the moment, there is no one discipline dominant in the higher posts, apart from dominance of specific disciplines within units of an apparently specialist nature.

Post entry training programs, offering general management and policy-oriented courses, are attracting increasing numbers of current civil servants. They are often presented as aiming at a strengthening of the generalist qualities of higher officials and to compensate for specialist orientations in academic education. There is more sympathy for the idea that postentry training should not be of an ad hoc and incidental nature, but part of an "éducation permanente" during an entire government career. Training programs are coordinated by the central State Training Institute (now privatized), which has an advisory role in developing training policy and offers training programs itself. Training is voluntary and complementary to the courses set up by the individual departments. Departments are autonomous in their training policies. Training is not yet seen as a prime necessity within the bureaucratic context. Therefore, there is also no automatic relation between training and career progression.

Departments, in order to meet their educational needs, also make use of the services of commercial training institutes. Post-doctoral courses are provided by universities, competing with one another by offering titles like "Master of Public Administration" (indeed, in English). Numerous programs focus on management development. Policy sciences are part of the curriculum but are often with no specific training in evaluation methodology. The Ministry of Finance's Department of Policy Evaluation offers much-attended courses in *ex ante* and *ex post* evaluation.

When we turn to remuneration and career policies we can be short: there are no formal rewards for evaluation expertise in general. Natural exceptions are specialized research units in the ministries, research councils, and the Court of Audit. The organizational placement of the evaluation function does not follow one line: the majority of the departmental units that regard themselves as being engaged in evaluation are placed in a policy directorate; the smaller number are formed by staff and research units. Six ministries have central units involved in evaluation research among other tasks. One-third of departmental units conduct their evaluations internally; two-thirds of the evaluation studies are being contracted out (the contract partner being a private or academic person or institute). Apart from an engagement in actual evaluation research, departmental units have supportive and coordinative tasks in this field.

The number of evaluation studies initiated at the central government level has clearly been growing in the 1980s, indicating an increasing willingness to reflect upon the performance of a program or an administrative practice. This development is also indicated by explicit measures to ensure that an evaluation will take place in programs with a "plan" status, or in legislation with "sun-set" provisions. The Court of Audit study (Algemene Rekenkamer 1990) found that 944 studies had been carried out between 1987 and 1989. Of these reports, about half actually deserved to be called evaluations.

It is important to note that the Court of Audit, in its recent survey, pressed for clearer rules and procedures regarding evaluation tasks, in order to prevent an ad hoc policy with regard to the execution of evaluation research, and to promote utilization. Recently, the government, reacting to the Algemene Rekenkamer study, stated that it considered systematic and periodic policy evaluation of importance and phrased political intentions to stimulate and initiate policy evaluations by integrating it into departmental structures, the policy process, and the budgetary process. The Court of Audit itself is involved in evaluatory tasks both in the field of financial and of performance audit. The Department of Policy Evaluation and Instrumentation within the Ministry of Finance is engaged in consultation activities, the publication of guidelines for evaluation, and especially in educational activities. The department's approach in furthering the cause of policy evaluation is now favoring discretion on the part of the individual ministries.

For the Netherlands, we can conclude that the process of institutionalization of (*ex post*) evaluation is gradually reaching a phase where a more recognizable pattern presents itself. This development coincides with the growth to maturity of the subject in academic curricula, acquiring its full place in graduate programs in public administration and related curricula. In postentry training, the emphasis is on generalist qualities, which are also being understood to include a broad understanding of the policy process. The voluntary and decentralized character of training endeavors makes it difficult to relate training in the policy sciences to career progression, per se.

The open career system results in a fairly balanced representation of disciplines at the higher posts. The organizational placement of the evaluation function shows diversity in both staff and line positions. It is also present as an interdepartmental endeavor. Finally, it is important to note that a significant part of the actual evaluation research is being contracted out. Recent government declarations indicate at least a formal willingness to grant the evaluation function a more integrated part in the policy process.

The Scandinavian Countries

The Scandinavian countries offer a mixed picture. In Sweden, being one of the first wave countries, the evaluation function is well established. This is indicated by the efforts in ministries and agencies, the active role of the National Audit Office, of the Parliamentary Auditors, and of the ad hoc policy commissions. An interesting feature is the extensive consultation process with numerous stakeholders that takes place before the policy commission's proposals are reformulated into government draft bills and presented to Parliament (Vedung 1992).

Norway and Denmark are second wave countries. Both countries move in the direction of more goal- and result-oriented management, and toward a more explicit client orientation, which has induced increased attention for evaluation problems within and outside the administration. It seems that in Finland, so far, program evaluation is not standard practice although the new 1988 Budget Act formally introduced the evaluation function (Ahonen and Tammelin 1991).

Sweden has played a leading role (comparative to that of the United States) in the Scandinavian context (see also chapter 2, in this volume). Regretfully, we have little data on evaluation courses offered by universities and other institutes. There are, however, in the universities what might be called schools of public administration where policy evaluation is being taught. In the spring of 1991, a master's program for the training of civil servants was initiated by the Ministry of Public Administration as part of its general efforts to trim and modernize the public sector. This program, in which the major universities participate, also includes courses on evaluation theory and methodology.

In Norway and Denmark, evaluation-related blocks are offered in courses on public administration, political science, economics. and statistics. Occasionally, evaluation is taught as a subject in its own right. In Finland modules on policy analysis, evaluation, and implementation research were only recently introduced in academic public administration programs, while in related modules (on financial administration and government auditing) economic analysis and auditing are covered. Regular economics curricula do give students knowledge and analytic capabilities relevant for policy analysis and evaluation, but the subject as such is not represented.

In the Scandinavian countries, there is a great deal of movement between local government and central government and between the private and the public sector (Kingdom 1990: 153). The idea of civil service as a lifetime occupation does not apply. Therefore, what we are addressing are open career systems. Selection criteria are of a general nature: educational background, previous experience, oral/ written communication skills, and personal characteristics.

With the exception of a few services, such as the foreign service, recruitment to the administration normally does not involve particular examinations; interviews with candidates before final selection are standard. Evaluatory expertise normally does not carry any more weight than other qualifications, apart from specialist posts in the field. The resulting picture in Norway is one of an evenly spread representation of the disciplines: law, 24 percent; social sciences, 18 percent; economics, 16 percent; and engineering, 17 percent.

The Swedish bureaucracy seems to favor a degree in law as an entry qualification. Despite the growth in the number of people trained in other disciplines like economics and political science, and the increased importance of scientific and technological expertise, the proportion of civil service entrants with legal training is still more than half (Kingdom 1990: 152). In the case of Sweden this apparently has not hindered the introduction of evaluation expertise. But since we have no information on recruitment, career, and training policies, we shall not hazard an explanation.

Although in Finland there is a persistent strong position of lawyers in the ministries, recent studies suggest that their position is waning in terms of their total numbers. Social scientists (public administration, economics, political science) have recently gained ground. The typical education of department and agency personnel engaged in evaluation is either economics or social science (sociology, social policy, statistics, political science, public administration). Those staff with public administration training (the first academic program in public administration in Finland started in 1965) have definitely increased their numbers.

The introduction of result-oriented management is reflected via courses offered through in-house training programs. In Norway, various in-house courses and seminars are organized by the directorate of personnel, and by the ministries themselves, dealing with subjects like goal- and result-oriented management, *ex ante* evaluation, decision making processes, and so on. The supply of these training programs was stimulated by a Royal Decree in 1985 introducing *ex ante* evaluation to accompany legislation, regulations, reports, and propositions to Parliament.

The Danish central training institute, the Danish School of Public Administration, provides training for government officials at all levels. It offers an eight-week course in top management covering subjects related to evaluation (European Institute of Public Administration [EIPA] 1985). As in other countries, the role of training in the different departments varies very much in Denmark. There was in 1985 a general trend toward a more systematic training policy connected with the program of modernization of the public sector that encouraged departments to stimulate training activities.

The Finnish government also has a central unit for civil service training with consulting and training duties. Large agencies typically have training units of their own. Courses on policy analysis and evaluation (including cost-benefit analysis and auditing) are given. Central government organizations need not make exclusive use of this center's training programs. They may also buy training services from outside contractors. Both Norwegian and Finnish government organizations do not sanction evaluation expertise either positively or negatively. Such expertise carries no more weight than other qualifications where remuneration and promotion are concerned.

In Sweden, the evaluation of program effects is undertaken by the ministries and by agencies as well as by Sweden's unique sector-oriented research councils and research bodies, by independent researchers, by universities, by private consultants, by the National Audit Bureaus' Performance Auditing Department, and by government committees. In the three-year budget cycle that began in 1991,

> all agencies are required to submit a triennial in-depth appropriations request accompanied by among other things an analysis of results, comprising an account of the agency's achievements during the preceding five year period. In short, agencies will be expected to follow up and evaluate their activities. (Sandahl 1992)

How this will work out in actual practice still remains to be seen, especially because of the agencies' lack of sufficient expertise to conduct evaluations. In the meantime a critical review by the Parliamentary Auditors has revealed that actual practice does differ from intentions (Riksdagens Revisorer 1991).

The organizational placement of the evaluation function in Norway is such that, apart from the Foreign Ministry, ministries do not have separate units engaged in evaluation. Evaluation is carried out in conjunction with other tasks like budgeting or planning. Concentrated evaluatory efforts on a one-time basis may take the form of project groups. Evaluation activities that serve government agencies are concentrated in the nongovernmental research sector. Thus, the Research Center for Organization and Management is an independent institution established to carry out evaluation research, with an interdisciplinary emphasis, focusing on processes of change and adaptation in organizations and in society.

There is no regular place for the evaluation function in the Finnish national government. A central functional unit in the prime minister's office was recently (1991) transferred to the Ministry of the Interior, resulting in an emphasis on regional planning. At the Ministry of Finance there is an Economic Planning Center engaged in evaluation-type forecasting projects. The unit did not realize the centralized steering function originally intended, and thus evaluation as an essential part of the sectorial planning system failed. In addition, some evaluation-related functions persist in some of the ministries, especially those dealing with health, social welfare, and education. With the new 1988 Budget Act, aiming at establishing a system of result-oriented management and budgeting, the cause of program evaluation seems to have been furthered (Ahonen and Tammelin 1991). This is indicated by an increase of evaluative information provided to Parliament, the activities of the State Audit Office in the performance auditing field, as well as by the recent reorientation in the work of the parliamentary auditors to include program evaluation in their efforts.

The Scandinavian countries are open to the management philosophies involving an orientation on evaluation, although in different degrees, Sweden having the lead. Evaluation as a subject was originally being taught in the context of academic programs in economics, sociology, and political science, but gradually acquired a place of its own especially in public administration programs. In-house training programs attune themselves to the new-felt needs: courses on policy analysis and evaluation are now represented. The organizational placement has taken a firm form in Sweden, but is still rather scattered in Norway and Finland. We conclude that, in general, there is a correspondence between the degree of institutionalization and the degree to which HRM expresses the acknowledgment of evaluation as a tool of public management.

Great Britain

In Great Britain, an administrative "ethos more like that of the senior common room in one of the older universities than of the board rooms of the twentieth-century industry which shapes the environment of modern government" has, in the view of Kingdom (1990: 29), hindered the introduction of modern managerial concepts, particularly in the higher levels. After attempts at rationalization of the Public Expenditure Process (PES) via Program Analysis and Review (PAR), the Thatcher government sought a reorientation to focus on "cash management" and the control of resources rather than on any idea of program output and impact. Administrative reforms were introduced under the heading of the "Efficiency Strategy" and the "Financial Management Initiative."

Evaluation efforts associated with these strategies (clearly defined objectives and the means to measure outputs and performance in relation to these objectives) ended in performance measures of a rather shallow nature dominated by input rather than output data (Jenkins and Gray 1990, 1992). The most recent program "The Next Steps" centers on the creation of "agencies" that are freestanding and headed by a chief executive who, within a policy and resources framework set by departments, would have considerable powers over personnel management and finances. Where these agencies are expected to be accountable, evaluation comes in. In the effort, "evaluation and the institutions through which it was carried out acquired a new and more sharply defined public profile" in the 1980s (Henkel 1991: 9).

It is difficult to give a good overview of the state of affairs so far as evaluation is concerned. There is the division between central and local government that hinders a crisp assessment. For example, education, health, housing, and social services are, in the main, delivered and administered by local government or bodies like health authorities. Recent developments make the picture even more complex, like the fragmentation of civil service activities in Next Steps agencies. The National Audit Office (central government) and the Audit Commission (local government) are the first and foremost audit bodies. Since 1983, there has been a stronger role for the National Audit Office, which, in cooperation with the Public Accounts Committee (PAC), has the right also to examine economy, efficiency, and effectiveness issues. The Audit Commission was created in 1982 to monitor and promote economy, efficiency, and effectiveness in local management.

Of the Whitehall departments, some conduct evaluative reviews under their own initiative and some hire consultants to undertake studies. The use of management consultants in central government departments substantially increased in the 1980s (Henkel 1991). Others may fund academic research from universities or research institutes. However, most of this commissioned work is ad hoc and fragmentary. More importantly, much of it remains classified and unpublished, which also goes for other government-initiated evaluations (Jenkins 1989.) Classical inspections and advisory services like the Social Service

Inspectorate and the Health Advisory Service are expected to strengthen their evaluative capacities (Henkel 1991: 92).

The fragmentation in terms of decentralization, privatization, and agency formation and the ensuing autonomy in matters of internal management makes it also more difficult to draw a clear picture of civil service personnel practices. As for pre-entry socialization, we noted earlier the existence of schools of public policy on a considerable scale in the United States, indicating their perceived high relevance for public service, and the lack of equivalents in Britain (Bulmer 1987: 35).

Modules on policy analysis and evaluation probably are being presented in courses that have different names. There are degrees with titles such as Public Administration and Management (Kent) or Policy-Making and Administration (Essex). There are also a number of degrees in public administration in the polytechnics. At the postgraduate level there are one or two specialized master programs that may carry the term *policy* in their title. They, however, are mostly in-service courses. Other than these, the fashion is now for master's programs in Public Sector Management or more general MBA programs. It is "management" rather than "policy" that course designers are stressing and students seem to seek. Oxford and Cambridge have never been concerned with offering "policy analysis related courses" though they are both now quite keen on developing management and MBA programs.

Selection criteria for entrance in terms of educational background indicate that, apart from the well-commented "Oxbridge bias," there is no systematic education system for senior civil servants (Kingdom 1990: 23). In the early 1970s, only 3 percent of the civil service elite had a law degree, and 12 percent graduated in social sciences. British bureaucrats were particularly likely to have studied humanities, and (second to the United States) technology, and natural sciences (26 percent) (Aberbach et al. 1981: 51–53). Campbell (1983) mentions 17 percent for the social sciences for the early 1980s, so there seems to be a slight increase in their representation.

The variety in recruitment mechanisms once again presents a complex picture. Central to the recruitment process is the Civil Service Commission and its task of recruiting "high flyers" into the civil service as administrative trainees. This process is conducted first via generalist examinations and then via interviews and selection boards. However, most of the recruitment for lower grades is being done by the departments themselves. Admissions procedures and qualifications have been a matter for the department and the Civil Service Commission. Further, all recruitment below Grade 7 (Principal Level) has been handed over to departments and the new agencies. This leaves the commissioners responsible for only administrative trainee recruitment and recruitment to senior posts at Grade 7 and above (i.e., 5 percent or less of all civil service recruitment).

How does postentry training open up for policy science related themes? "Perhaps the most prominent feature of the British tradition of civil service training is that there is not very much of it, at least in any formal sense" (Drewry and Butcher, 1988: 110). In a survey of the situation in 1985, the EIPA states that civil servants have the opportunity to choose between training provided either by the departments themselves, the Civil Service College, or external training institutes. In general, the role of the Civil Service College seems marginal: government departments are not required to use the college courses and they must pay tuition for all courses attended by their staff. Primary responsibility for the training of their employees lies with the government departments. The types of training range from introductory training for entrants, mid-career training to improve work performance and develop potential, to development training in preparation of different and more senior jobs. Training is, however, mainly vocational in nature (job-specific functional training), while management and supervisory training accounted for only 12 percent of the training in 1985. As for management training that might provide modules on evaluation, it is mainly provided by departments (80 percent), while 5 percent is provided by external institutions and 15 percent by the Civil Service College. The college's management courses include modules on the policy process, efficiency and effectiveness in government, and operations research.

There is no formal connection between training and career progression. Selection boards usually decide on promotion to higher positions on the basis of interviews and of staff reports that record performance on-the-job, relative strengths and weaknesses, and longer-term potentials.

We have looked earlier at the organizational placement of the evaluation function. Its place at the central government level is, once again, not easily characterized because departments differ markedly in how they are organized and operate. The "evaluator" is not identifiable because it is not an official grade or job description. Departments, however, would claim to do evaluations. The groups who do this would include or involve professional grades such as economists, statisticians, computer experts, and generalist administrators. Therefore, arrangements will vary from project to project and department to department.

Although starting off with several rather grand-scheme endeavors, evaluation has had trouble finding a firm place in British government. Its institutionalization has been made more difficult by a traditional administrative culture, which is also expressed in HRM policies. Structural developments like the trend toward decentralization and self-control make a firm central grip on developments more difficult, unless the new freedom obtained is conditioned by the outcome of evaluations. There, the picture is not conclusive yet, as it is in so many other countries.

France

Although political and economic factors have not differed much from other countries over the past two decades, France has shown a reluctant interest in evaluation. In 1985, Nioche and Poinsard drew the following picture: "Although the signs of development are evident—increasing numbers of evaluations, aroused public and parliamentary interest, active administrative involvement—the process is not uniform, codified, or generally rigorous. Evaluations show poor quality" (1985: 58).

Existing evaluation efforts remain essentially compliance controls, the "inspections" emphasize verification of adherence to regulations and procedures, and implement what is essentially a financial audit (Quermonne and Rouban 1986: 402). The same qualification applies to the Cour des Comptes. Recent indications of concern for evaluation are "less the result of a coherent policy than they are isolated initiatives aiming to go beyond the traditional financial control function to which the bulk of the office's resources are devoted" (Nioche and Poinsard 1985: 64). The absence of any institution in France specifically devoted to the appraisal of public policy and the lack of a formal recognition, or put differently, the lack of institutionalization, reinforced the lack of appreciation.

Officials . . . do not assign their most effective resources to the evaluative endeavor, or such resources are inadequately applied. In turn, the results of the evaluation are less illuminating and useful than they might be. Accordingly, the evaluation process fails to gain structure and acceptance. (Nioche and Poinsard 1985: 61–63)

In 1986, 74 percent of all evaluation projects emanated from the bureaucracy, especially from the various ministries, the powerful Planning Commissariat and the Finance Ministry's Forecasting Commission. Sixteen percent came from research centers and only 0.5 percent from private consulting firms. These evaluation projects have insufficient implementation validity and therefore show little connection with the decision making process. The creation in 1983 of the Parliamentary Office for Assessment of Scientific and Technological Choice introduced *ex-ante* evaluation, and as such was a "first step towards the institutionalization of an evaluation system" (Quermonne and Rouban 1986: 402).

Still, the mismatch between the actual administrative philosophies and the increasingly perceived needs and wants with which the government was confronted could well have started a double-loop learning process. Commentators note that the impetus that could have triggered this were factors of the same nature as elsewhere: budgetary problems, increased government intervention in new policy fields, combined with a growing public resistance against government interventions. In this context, evaluation could be presented as an instrument to inform the public and to increase effectiveness in an attempt to modernize the state, and in the new search for political and administrative accountability (Quermonne and Rouban 1986: 397–8). The question here is why this has not occurred.

Quermonne and Rouban (1986: 404) point to cultural traditions, a political process little involved in acquiring an "information-based consensus," and an administrative ideology shared by civil servants that rests upon the institutional role of the "Grands Corps" and the crucial weight of administrative law. They point to "the real influence of administrative law upon all aspects of public administration." Civil servants have been trained in this legalistic tradition and are poorly informed about the new methods of policy science. Given this shared "theory-in-use," a new approach less regulated by law, may appear controversial, even dangerous. Thus, double-loop learning is blocked.

Quermonne and Rouban's main thesis is "that policy evaluation implies a logic of integration which differs radically from the present one in France" (1986: 404).

Pre-entry socialization confirms the picture. The route to the top of the French civil service is well known to be narrow, a road along certain schools (Institutes of Political Studies) ending with the ENA (École National d'Administration). The ENA offers general training. The aim of the education is not to produce a generalist in the British sense of the word, but rather to produce "a non-technical administrator" (Kingdom 1990: 76–77). Only in the past few years has the ENA begun to provide management-training courses with subjects like the management of public organizations, management techniques, public decision-making, and policy implementation (EIPA 1985).

As for recruitment and career policies, "the most prestigious and powerful career avenues in the administration run through the grands corps, and the most strategically crucial sectors of the administration are—if not in law then certainly in fact—the property of those corps" (Kingdom 1990: 74). It is clear that the Grands Corps and the association of elite administrators within the civil service[6] share a common preparation and training and a common grade structure. As such it holds the relevant positive sanctions for the ambitious civil servant.

In 1990, substantial new initiatives were taken to grant evaluation a formal place in the administrative process (Nioche 1992). A three-tiered system has been created: an Interministerial Committee of Evaluation presided over by the prime minister and composed of principal ministers, a National Fund for the Development of Evaluations, and a Scientific Evaluation Board.

The interministerial committee is responsible for developing and coordinating government evaluation initiatives. It orders interdepartmental evaluation projects, as well as projects using a fund specifically for evaluation studies. Suggestions for evaluation studies can be submitted to the committee by various administrative audit, monitoring or socioeconomic planning organizations. The committee is also responsible for approving the modalities of studies, in particular the criteria for the selection of the individuals, public or private, who will conduct the evaluation.

The National Fund for the Development of Evaluation supports evaluations approved by the interdepartmental committee. The third organization, the Scientific Evaluation Board, consists of eleven individuals appointed by the prime minister to a six-year non-renewable term. The members are selected on the basis of their expertise in the field of evaluation, economics, sociology, or administration. Their mandate is to promote the development of evaluation methods, to define a code of ethics for the evaluation profession, and to ensure the quality and objectivity of studies approved by the interdepartmental committee.

Very recently, this "Counseil Scientifique de l'Évaluation" issued its first Rapport Annuel (1991) on evaluation practices, giving a good overview of the state of affairs (characterized by the authors with "dynamisme et faiblesses") and the challenges to be met. In general they found that "la fonction évaluative est désormais identifiée en tant que telle." They point at specialist administrative units within departments and independent bodies, all created after 1984, with missions in the field of evaluation. The report also notes new initiatives at regional and local levels. They also point to the growing willingness of the Cour des Comptes to engage in performance audits. The board feels that evaluation is more and more considered to be a mission inherent to the responsibility of managers of public funds.

In spite of the present uncommonly large degree of political support, there remain the factors that may impede the development of a healthy evaluation function in France. The elite of the French Public Service, who are part of the government's Grands Corps, appear not to have been involved in the evaluation reform. They, the "Inspection des Finances" and the Cour des Comptes "may well view evaluation as a competitor and perhaps wish to derail it" (Lemay 1991).

In the light of our working hypothesis that HRM has a role to play in creating the climate for the acceptance and practice of evaluation as a tool of organizational learning, developments in France are most illuminating. They illustrate a process of acceptance that had to break through a dominant administrative culture and a correspondingly tight structure. HRM policies reflect this process of hesitant acceptance. The recent major political backing could initiate several innovative developments. If, however, actual policies in the field of HRM are not supportive of that innovation, the development of the evaluation function may be impeded to the degree that it will eventually end in frustration.

Conclusion

We have looked first at the evidence from ten countries for HRM as an instrument for single-loop learning. Here the question is whether HRM, as an expression of the administrative philosophy, actually reflects the state of affairs with regard to the evaluation function. Second, we have sought to address the issue of HRM as a facilitator for double-loop learning through evaluation. Does HRM reflect appreciation for variety and new perspectives? Or does it only represent dominant administrative views and therefore hinder the development and implementation of new models and paradigms such as implied by double-loop learning?

Our task was complicated by (apart from limited availability of data) the fact that there appears to be a decentralizing trend with respect to HRM in almost all countries. This development is concomitant with the "retreat-of-state" movement leaving departments, agencies, and local government with an increasing policy discretion in HRM as in other functions. Fluxion in the HRM response to evaluation is inevitable.

The ten countries have also been categorized by the two "waves" in accepting evaluation as a relevant tool of public management. It is obvious that with the first wave countries, the United States and Canada in particular, the well-established place for evaluation in central government has been supported and facilitated by the advanced training offered in the field as well as by an administrative culture open to innovative ideas. This is illustrated by the career system and a strong representation of the relevant sciences.

The early but reluctant efforts at evaluation in Germany are explained by political and constitutional factors, by a legalistic administrative culture and a generalist notion of administrative judgment. HRM policies reflect this state of affairs, although recent studies indicate a growing acknowledgment of the value of evaluation.

In the Netherlands, pre-entry socialization in academic training and the introduction of the evaluation function on a systematic scale have gone hand-in-hand. A long period of incubation was needed in the 1970s and a changing political and economic climate to induce the institutionalization, which is typical for the second wave countries. HRM tools do not reflect a dominant administrative philosophy nor a traditional view of officialdom.

Facilitating Organizational Learning 179

Within the Scandinavian countries the various waves in the institutionalization process are represented. The forward position of Sweden is somewhat difficult to relate to its HRM because we lack most of the relevant data. It has had an early willingness to introduce new budgeting (PPBS) and management concepts. Developments in Norway and Denmark resemble those in the Netherlands, although the integration of the evaluation function is less clear. Finland seems to be coming along rather carefully, but clearly in the direction of institutionalizing evaluation within central government.

All Scandinavian countries offer evaluation-related modules in their academic courses either in the context of economics or political science or in the relatively new master's programs in public administration. This development is apparently of a recent nature. The open career systems favor general selection criteria. In Finland and Sweden the jurist still holds a firm though waning position. The social sciences and economics are gaining ground. In Norway and Denmark academic disciplines are rather evenly represented. Efforts to introduce result-oriented management concepts are reflected in the programs of in-house training, offering management courses with modules covering evaluation. Thus, what we find is a different pace in development of evaluation functions reflected in HRM policies as well.

In Great Britain the administrative ethos has created difficulties for the introduction of modern management concepts. The attempts at evaluation, however, have been manyfold since the 1970s and are still going on under different headings. HRM policies offer an inconclusive picture. Pre-entry training in evaluation seems not to have an explicit place of its own in academic curricula, although it might go under different banners. The social sciences are underrepresented in the higher civil service, though their proportion is increasing. Otherwise, there are no clear indications of appreciation of evaluation expertise outside specialist functions.

France is the example par excellence of what we might call a "third wave country" as far as the institutionalization of evaluation is concerned. Double-loop learning, and therefore innovation, are hampered by a dominant administrative culture of a legalistic nature. This is well illustrated by training, recruitment, and career policies still serving the traditional view of officialdom and a structure linked with vital interests.

Our evidence suggests that there is an interesting degree of correspondence between the pace in the institutionalization of evaluation and the degree to which the dominant administrative philosophies, expressed in HRM policies, are open to innovation. Where the administrative-legal culture is clearly dominant and HRM is hesitant (or repressed) in expressing different values and academic specialties, the acknowledgment of evaluation is seriously hindered. This correspondence may indicate a conditional relationship: the clear need for HRM to support and facilitate the introduction of evaluation into central government as an innovation. This idea is not new, of course, and is well documented in innovation literature (Merritt and Merritt 1985).

There are a number of developments in the sphere of HRM that the countries we studied share:

- An open recruitment and career system is conditional for double-loop learning. The countries with the greatest diversity in this respect have had a leading role.
- In all countries where the jurists have dominated the policy arena, we find evidence for their gradual retreat in favor of the social sciences (economists, political scientists, sociologists) and more recently by graduates from public administration programs. In general, there is a growing diversification in the representation of disciplines, also at the highest administrative levels.
- Missing education in the policy sciences is increasingly being supplemented in postentry training, first of all by the agencies appealing to specialist evaluation expertise, like auditing bodies, but also in management course offerings where it is being taught at a general level.
- It has been difficult to determine whether evaluation expertise is being specifically rewarded. There is too great a diversity in organizational placement (line, staff, committee formulas, semigovernmental research bodies, etc.) and the function of "evaluator" as such is often difficult to identify, since the art goes under many different names.
- Remuneration and career policies seem to suggest that evaluation expertise and its utilization are mainly rewarded in relation to specialist functions within the organization.

We conclude that in pre- and postentry socialization evaluation expertise is on the one hand increasingly appreciated as a specialist skill and the utilization of evaluation information as an ingredient (of a specialist nature) in general administrative judgment. On the other hand, it is more and more being perceived as part of the generalist and managerial tool kit of the higher executive, given its intimate relation to the chief functions of management and administration. Here the work of Gray, Jenkins, and Segsworth (1993) is especially informative on the interrelations of budgeting, auditing, and evaluation. In the end, this development may hold the greatest promise. If it is appreciated as a relevant policy tool by the leading officials, they will be more inclined to ask for evaluation expertise in their organization, thus starting an accumulation process. Our prognosis would be that as evaluators grow in numbers, not only in specialist posts where there is an appeal for their specific skills, but also in the leading, generalist posts, the acceptance and actual use of evaluation will grow. This acceptance, in itself an example of successful double-loop learning, will bring the lasting challenge for evaluation to prove its instrumentality for organizational learning.

Notes

1. HRM is not an unequivocal concept. Its premises need continual testing, especially the premise that the interpretation of personnel management and labor relations in the light of the organizational objectives are without problems (Kluytmans and Paauwe 1991). In the period under study in this article, HRM philosophies were probably only applied to a limited degree. We use the concept here in an analytical sense, since it expresses the integration of the organization's strategy and personnel management.
2. Ideally, we should research how much these professionals still see themselves as professionally linked to their discipline and are engaged as such via role orientation and work experience. Research into different professional languages, repertoires, appreciative systems, role patterns, and so on should shed light on their influence on policy-making, political competition among varying professional appreciative systems, as well as competition between political ideologies and professional appreciations (e.g., the preference of social democrat governments for social-science research). This kind of research would be all the more interesting, since "literature shows little concern either with historic change in the implicit model which may have dominated government arrangements or concerns, or with the possibility that variations in culture, policy system or social science traditions may give rise to significant variations between nations" (Blume in Bulmer 1987: 77).
3. Relevant data were collected for: the United States by E.N. Goldenberg, R.C. Rist, and R. Sonnichsen; Canada by J. Mayne and R.V. Segsworth; Sweden by E. Vedung; Norway by B. Eriksen; Finland by P. Ahonen; the Netherlands by M.L. Bemelmans-Videc; Great Britain by W.I. Jenkins; and Germany by H. U. Derlien.
4. Focused on specific groups of potential entrants are programs in the United States like: (1) the Presidential Management Intern Program, which provides for an

annual hiring of 200 to 400 individuals who have completed master's degree requirements in the fields of public management or public policy; and (2) the Cooperative Education Programs designed for undergraduate and graduate students offering alternate periods of study and education-related work experience.
5. The Office of the Comptroller General is responsible for financial management in the federal government and is part of the Treasury Board. The Treasury Board is the committee of ministers responsible for budgeting and administration in the federal government.
6. The Grands Corps may be divided into the technical corps, such as Mining Engineering, Rural Engineering, Bridges and Highways, and the nontechnical such as the Council of State, Court of Accounts, Finance Inspectorate, the Diplomatic Corps, and the Prefectoral Corps.

References

Aberbach, J.D., R.D. Putnam, and B.A. Rockman. 1981. *Bureaucrats and Politicians in Western Democracies.* Cambridge, MA: Harvard University Press.

Ahonen, P., and E. Tammelin. 1991. "Evaluative Auditing of Budgeting in the Finnish Central Government." Paper prepared for the IIAS Working Group on Policy Evaluation. Brugge, Belgium.

Argyris, C., and D.A. Schön. 1978. *Organizational Learning; A Theory of Action Perspective.* Reading, MA: Addison-Wesley.

Algemene Rekenkamer. 1990.*Verslag 1990.* TK 22032, 1–2. The Hague: Algemene Rekenkamer.

Armstrong, J.A. 1973. *The European Administrative Elite.* Princeton, NJ: Princeton University Press.

Bemelmans-Videc, M.L. 1990. "Dutch Experience in the Utilization of Evaluation Research; The Procedure of Reconsideration." *Knowledge in Society* 2, no. 4: 31–48.

———. 1992. "Institutionalizing Evaluation: An International Perspective." In *Advancing Public Policy Evaluation: Learning from International Experiences,* ed. J. Mayne, M.K. Bemelmans-Videc, J. Hudson, and R. Conner. Amsterdam: Elsevier Science Publishers.

Blume, S.S. 1987. "Social Science in Whitehall: Two Analytic Perspectives." In *Social Science Research and Government: Comparative Essays on Britain and the U.S.,*.ed. M. Bulmer. Cambridge, England: Cambridge University Press.

Bourgault, J., and S. Dion. 1991. *The Changing Profile of Federal Deputy Ministers 1867 to 1988.* Canadian Center for Management Development, Ottawa.

Bulmer, M. 1987. *Social Science Research and Government: Comparative Essays on Britain and the U.S.* Cambridge, England: Cambridge University Press.

Campbell, C. 1983. *Governments under Stress: Political Executives and Key Bureaucrats in Washington, London and Ottawa.* Toronto: University of Toronto Press.

Campbell, C., and G. Szablowski. 1979. *The Superbureaucrats.* Toronto: Macmillan.

Canadian Evaluation Society. 1990. *"National Inventory of Academic and Training Courses,"* Ottawa.

Chandler, R.C. 1987. *A Centennial History of the American Administrative State.* New York: The Free Press.

Chelimsky, E., 1987. *Federal Evaluation: Fewer Units, Reduced Resources, Different Studies from 1980.* GAO-Program Evaluation and Methodology Division, General Accounting Office/PEMD-87–9.

Cleary, R.E. 1989. "What Do Public Administration Masters Programs Look Like These Days?" A preliminary report. (unpublished).

Comptroller General of Canada. 1990. *Program Evaluation Newsletter.* No. 23. Ottawa, Canada: Program Evaluation Branch, Comptroler General of Canada.

Conseil Scientifique de l'Évaluation. 1991. *L'Évaluation de l'expertise à la responsabilité.* Rapport Annuel sur l'évolution des pratiques d'évaluation des politiques. publiques. Paris: CSE.

Derlien, H.U. 1985. "Politicization of the Civil Service in the Federal Republic of Germany—Facts and Fables" In *La Politisation de l'Administration,* ed. F. Meyers. Brussels: IIAS.

———. *Changes in Ten Executives,* CESSI-project Study 2, ongoing.

———. 1988. "Repercussions of Government Change on the Career Civil Service in West Germany: The Cases of 1969 and 1982." *Governance: An International Journal of Policy and Administration.* 1, no. 1: 50–78.

———. 1989a. "Keeping the Balance between Political Appointments and Professional Careers—the Case of the FRG." Paper presented at the XXIst International Congress of Administative Sciences, Marrakech.

———. 1989b. "A Longitudinal Study of the West German Federal Elite: Methodology and Findings of Two Recent Projects." In *Institutions and Bureaucrats,* ed. S. Tiihonen. Helsinki: Government Printing Center.

———. 1990a. "Genesis and Structure of Evaluation Efforts in Comparative Perspective." In Ray C. Rist, *Program Evaluation and the Management of Government: Patterns and Prospects across Eight Nations.* New Brunswick, NJ: Transaction Publishers.

———. 1990b. "Program Evaluation in the Federal Republic of Germany." In Ray C. Rist, *Program Evaluation and the Management of Government: Patterns and Prospects across Eight Nations,* ed. Ray L. Rist. New Brunswick, NJ: Transaction Publishers.

Drewry, G., and T. Butcher. 1988. *The Civil Service Today.* Oxford: Blackwell.

European Institute of Public Administration. 1985. *Training Civil Servants in Europe*. Maastricht, Netherlands: EIPA.

Feldman, M.S., and J.G. March. 1981. "Information in Organizations as Signal and Symbol." *Administrative Science Quarterly* 26: 171–86.

Ferrari, V. 1990. "Socio-Legal Concepts and Their Comparison." In *Comparative Methodology; Theory and Practice in International Social Research*, ed. E. Oyen, 63–80. London: Sage.

Fesler, J.W. 1987. "The Higher Public Service in Western Europe." In *A Centennial History of the American Administrative State*, ed. R.C. Chandler. New York: The Free Press.

Fesler, J.W., and D.F. Kettl. 1991. *The Politics of the Administrative Process*. Chatham, NJ: Chatham House Publishers.

General Accounting Office. 1982. *A Profile of Federal Program Evaluation Activities*. GAO Institute for Program Evaluation: Special Study I. Washington, DC: U.S. General Accounting Office.

———. 1988. *Program Evaluation Issues. Office of the Comptroller General*. GAO/OCG-89–8TR. Washington, DC: U.S. General Accounting Office.

Gray, A., A.W. Jenkins, and R.V. Segsworth, eds. 1993. *Budgeting, Auditing and Evaluation: Functions and Integration in Seven Governments*. New Brunswick, NJ: Transaction Publishers.

Hedberg, B. 1981. "How Organizations Learn and Unlearn." In *Handbook of Organizational Design.* ed. P.C. Nystrom and W.H. Starbuck, 3–27. New York: Oxford University Press.

Hellstern, G.M., and H. Wollmann. 1989. "Evaluation in the Federal Republic of Germany." Working document. IIAS/FUCAM, Brussels/Mons.

Henkel, M. 1991. *Government, Evaluation and Change*. London: Jessica Kingsley Publishers.

Henry, N. 1987. "The Emergence of Public Administration as a Field of Study." In *A Centennial History of the American Administrative State*, ed. R.C. Chandler, 37–85. New York: The Free Press.

Hodgkinson, C. 1982. *Towards a Philosophy of Administration*. Oxford: Blackwell.

Jann, W. 1991. "From Policy Analysis to Political Management? An Outside Look at Public-Policy Training in the United States." In *Social Sciences and Modern States: National Experiences and Theoretical Crossroads*, ed. P. Wagner, C. Weiss, B. Wittrock, and H. Wollmann. Cambridge, England: Cambridge University Press.

Jenkins, W.I. 1989. *Policy Evaluation in the UK: Its Development and Impact on Citizen-Clients*. Working Document. Brussels/Mons: IIAS/FUCAM.

Jenkins, W.I., and A. Gray. 1990. "Policy Evaluation in British Government: From Idealism to Realism?" In R.C. Rist, *Program Evaluation and the Management of Government: Patterns and Prospects across Eight Nations*, ed. R.C. Rist. New Brunswick, NJ: Transaction Publishers.

———. 1992. "Evaluation and the Consumer: The UK Experience." In *Advancing Public Policy Evaluation: Learning from International Experiences*, ed. J. Mayne, M.L. Bemelmans-Videc, J. Hudson, and R. Conner. Amsterdam: Elsevier Science Publishers.

Kernaghan, K., and P.K. Kuruvilla. 1980. "Merit and Motivation: Public Personnel Management in Canada." In *Canadian Public Administration: Discipline and Profession*, ed. K. Kernaghan. Toronto: Publisher?

Kingdom, J.E., ed. 1990. *The Civil Service in Liberal Democracies; An Introductory Survey*. London: Routledge.

Kluytmans, F., and J. Paauwe. 1991. "HRM denkbeelden: De balans opgemaakt." In *M&O Tijdschrift voor Organisatiekunde en Sociaal Beleid*, ed. Insert editor(s), 279–303. City: Publishers?

Leeuw, F., and H.C.D. Boer. 1989. "Regierungspolitik und Policy-Forschung in den Niederlanden." *Jahrbuch zur Staats- und Verwaltungswissenschaft*, ed. ?, 291–314. Baden-Baden: Publisher?

Lemay, M. 1991. "The Evaluation of Public Policies in France." In *Program Evaluation Newsletter*, no. 27. Program Evaluation Branch, Comptroller General of Canada, 5–8.

Leviton, L.C., and E.F.X. Hughes. 1981. "Research on the Utilization of Evaluations; A Review and Synthesis." *Evaluation Review* 5, no. 4: 525–48.

McCurdy, H.E. 1986. *Public Administration: A Bibliographic Guide to the Literature*. New York: M. Dekker.

March, J.G., and J.P. Olsen. 1976. *Ambiguity and Choice in Organizations*. Bergen, Norway: Universitetsforlaget.

Mayne, J., M.L. Bemelmans-Videc, J. Hudson, and R. Conner. (Eds.). 1992. *Advancing Public Policy Evaluation: Learning from International Experiences*. Amsterdam: Elsevier Science Publishers.

Mény, Y. 1990. *Government and Politics in Western Europe; Britain, France, Italy, Germany*. Oxford: Oxford University Press.

Merritt, R.L., and A.J. Merritt, eds. 1985. *Innovation in the Public Sector*. Beverly Hills: Sage.

Nioche, J.P. 1992. "Evaluation in France." In *Advancing Public Policy Evaluation: Learning from International Experiences*, ed. J. Mayne, M.L. Bemelmans-Videc, J. Hudson, and R. Conner. Amsterdam: Elsevier Science Publishers.

Nioche, J.P., and R. Poinsard. 1985. "Public Policy Evaluation in France." *Journal of Policy Analysis and Management* 5, no. 1: 58–72.

Office of Personnel Management. 1988a. The Report of the President's Commission on Compensation of Career Federal Executives. Washington, DC: United States Government Printing Office.

———. 1988b. The Senior Executive Service, SES 88–01. Washington, DC: United States Government Printing Office.

———. 1988c. *A Profile of the Senior Executive Service*, OPM/Office of Executive Personnel. Washington, DC: United States Government Printing Office.

———. 1988/89. "In Search of Merit; Hiring Entry-Level Federal Employees." OPM/Oficer of Executive Personnel. Washington, DC: U.S. Government Printing Office.

Olsen, D. (1980). *The State Elite.* Toronto: McClelland and Stewart.

Oyen, E., ed. 1990. *Comparative Methodology; Theory and Practice in International Social Research.* London: Sage.

Quermonne, J.L., and L. Rouban. 1986. "French Public Administration and Policy Evaluation: The Quest for Accountability." *Public Administration Review* 46, no. 5: 397–406.

Ridley, F. 1979. *Government and Administration in Western Europe.* Oxford: University Press.

Riksdagens Revisorer. 1991. *Resultatorienterat Budgetarbete.* Rapport 1991/92:2, Stockholm: The Parliament.

Rist, R.C., ed. 1990. *Program Evaluation and the Management of Government: Patterns and Prospects across Eight Nations.* New Brunswick, NJ: Transaction Publishers.

Rohr, J.A. 1991. "Ethical Issues in French Public Administration: A Comparative Study," *Public Administation Review* 51, no. 4 (July/August): 283–97.

Sandahl, R. 1992. "Evaluation at the Swedish National Audit Bureau." In *Advancing Public Policy Evaluation: Learning from International Experiences,* ed. J. Mayne, M.L. Bemelmans-Videc, J. Hudson, and R. Conner. Amsterdam: Elsevier Science Publishers.

Segworth, R.V. 1990. "Policy and Program Evaluation in the Government of Canada." In *Program Evaluation and the Management of Government: Patterns and Prospects across Eight Nations,* ed. R.C. Rist. New Brunswick, NJ: Transaction Publishers.

Siedentopf, H., and C. Hauschild. 1988. "Personnel Policies in the Federal Republic of Germany: Scarce Resources and Modernization Programs." *International Review of Administrative Sciences* 54: 453–66.

Sonnichsen, R.C. 1988. "Advocacy Evaluation: A Model for Internal Evaluation Offices." *Evaluation and Program Planning* 11: 141–48.

———. 1989. "Program Managers: Victims or Victors in the Evaluation Process?" In *Evaluation and the Federal Decision Maker; New Directions for Program Evaluation,* no. 41, ed. G.L. Barkdoll. San Francisco: Jossey-Bass.

Storey, J., ed. 1989. *New Perspectives on Human Resource Management.* London: Routledge.

Treasury Board of Canada, Comptroller General. 1990. *Program Evaluation Newsletter,* no. 24 (March).

Vedung, E. 1992. "Five Observations on Swedish Evaluation." In *Advancing Public Policy Evaluation: Learning from International Experiences,* ed. J.

Mayne, M.L. Bemelmans-Videc, J. Hudson, and R. Conner. Amsterdam: Elsevier Science Publishers.
Vickers, Sir G. 1965. *The Art of Judgement: Policy Making as a Mental Skill.* London: Chapman and Hall.
Wagner, P., C. Hirschon Weiss, B. Wittrock, and H. Wollmann. 1991. *Social Sciences and Modern States. National Experiences and Theoretical Crossroads.* Cambridge, England: Cambridge University Press.
Wollmann, H. 1989. "Policy Analysis in West Germany's Federal Government: A Case of Unfinished Governmental and Administrative Modernization." *Governance, An International Journal of Policy and Administration* 2, no. 3 (July): 233–66.

8

The Preconditions for Learning: Lessons from the Public Sector

Ray C. Rist

The preceding chapters in this volume take as their point of departure the empirical question of whether it is possible to document the presence of organizational learning in the public sector. The answer is clearly answered and it is answered in the affirmative—organizational learning can be shown to exist in the public sector. It needs to be stressed that this is an answer of no small import, for the research to date in the area of organizational learning has been almost exclusively conducted within the private sector. Organizational learning has been a concept applied in the area of organizational analysis for the past forty years. Yet, the direct and systematic assessment of organizational learning in the public sector has been virtually nil.

Organizational learning happens among individuals. It is not a hypothetical or mystical event that has no grounding in the lives and experiences of human beings. It is not supernatural. It is linked to the biographies of the individuals within an organization, to the culture of the organization, to the styles of decision making, and to the means of communication (both formal and informal) within the organization. In sum, organizational learning takes place within the context of shared understandings, experiences, routines, values, and acceptable behaviors. Organizational learning does not take place among compete strangers. It cannot be programmed. It comes about in those settings where there is collective understanding of a situation, its presumed causes and its consequences, and the desire to change the present state or condition. Single-loop learning, as we have described, addresses ways of improving the present state of affairs, while double-loop learning brings about a fundamental reexamination of the condition and the current strategies to address it.

What makes the finding of organizational learning in the public sector even more significant is that in each and every instance, the studies collected here all document that the concept has vitality and applicability cross-nationally. It may be one thing to find an example of organizational learning in the context of a single government, but to have found clear instances of such learning taking place in varying governmental systems merits comment. The governmental systems studied here have produced information in quite different ways, processed it through their decision-making structures in country-specific fashion, and encouraged its use by persons of quite different training, and to different ends. These components all suggest the strength of the concept and its fruitfulness as a means of structuring comparative organizational analysis.

Further, and this is an additional unique contribution, the studies collected here show that a distinct form of information produced within governmental systems—program and policy evaluations—do contribute to organizational learning. The fact that public sector organizations produce large quantities of such information is not the same as saying that the information is then understood or acted upon by these same organizations. But it has been shown through these studies that governments do use this particular type of information in ways that enhance effectiveness and clearly contribute to successful governance. This is encouraging, and especially so for those who believe that governments must necessarily strive to constantly improve themselves.

Having opened this discussion on such a positive note, it is well to note several caveats. These are mentioned here at the beginning of the discussion in order to insure that the reader is aware of the constraints under which we worked to produce our research. First, we have been painfully aware of the limitations of both theory and research in the area of organizational learning. Our work in the theoretical literature as well as with the research reports on organizational learning both continually brought home the precarious nature of our endeavor. The present effort is not built on a deep foundation of extensive theory building and research on organizational learning. Indeed, Normann noted in 1985 that his assessment of the literature to date suggested that "surprisingly little systematic research and conceptualization have taken place in the area of organizational learning." Consequently, while the findings from the case studies in this volume both expand our theoretical understandings and deepen our research sophistication in studying empirically the concept of organizational learning in governmental systems, it is also the case that this is a first attempt to conduct such a large scale comparative assessment. Future research will have to refine and further define the nature of that learning and its subsequent impacts on governmental systems.

Second, the authors in this volume have used but one among many competing understandings of organizational learning. Taking as our point of departure the work of Argyris (discussed at some length in the Introduction), we have sought to frame our studies in terms of his concepts of single- and double-loop learning. This we have done and we feel we have clearly documented cases of both types of learning in the public sector. Yet it is also the case that there is no consensus on the definition of organizational learning. Duncan and Weiss (1979), Galagan (1989), Normann (1985), and Stata (1989) have all noted the variability in definitions. We recognize that from a different definition, our work may be challenged. We knew this from the beginning and decided to move ahead in any event, believing the Argyris definition was sufficiently intellectually robust to carry our comparative studies.

Third, the studies presented here do not give a comparative understanding of how evaluation and policy analysis influence organizational learning in contrast to, for example, the information gained from auditing or budgeting. Our work does not answer the question of the relative contribution that one might expect from different types of information produced within organizations. Thus, it is not possible to infer from this work the predisposition of an organization to accept one type of information more readily or with a higher degree of trustworthiness than another, or for that matter within empirical contexts of crisis.

Fourth, this present effort also does not answer the question of the relative existence of organizational learning in the public versus the private sector. Most of the research done to date has focused on the private sector. Blankenhagen (1992) nicely summarizes six surveys of the literature in organizational learning. The message from his metareview is clear—what we know of organizational learning is what we know from the private sector. Our studies all documented the presence of organizational learning in the public sector. We do not, however, know the extent of applicability of organizational learning in the private sector. Indeed, we cannot say whether the nature of the learning that takes place in these two domains is or is not similar, let alone whether the organizational processes that generate learning are or are not similar. Any comparisons at this point are tentative and extremely fragile.

It is important to note that the study of the contribution of policy and program evaluation information to organizational learning overlaps with but is not identical to the study of how social science research is or is not utilized in the public sector. There is a large and diverse literature on social science knowledge utilization, some subportion of which focuses on utilization in the public sector. This literature tends to address the ways in which social science research can contribute to governmental decision making. The differences between the study of organizational learning and that of social science utilization can be seen in the manner in which Chelimsky (1991: 226) has framed the question of why social science research frequently is not in a position to support the information needs of decision makers. Her answer goes in a very different direction from that which one would posit if the question were one of how to enhance organizational learning. She writes:

> What then are the kinds of mismatches that continue to prevent research from supporting decision needs appropriately? I see at least three: (i) when political requirements are so overwhelming that information simply will not be sought; (ii) when information is sought, but contextual or resource constraints on the analysis impede researchers from actually producing the information needed for the decision; and (iii) when "state of the art" research problems allow only inconclusive answers to decision-makers' questions. In any of these situations, there are constraints—either on the decision or on the research—that tend to prevent a match between the two from occurring.

The point in citing Chelimsky here is to note that the study of the (mis)match of research and decision making is not to be confused with the study of organizational learning. Organizational learning can come from many sources and via many avenues. Further, not all learning must necessarily drive or be associated with decision making. Decision making is but one among the multiple activities and functions of an organization. Learning can happen in and for the benefit of any organizational function.

The intent of my remarks is to identify those preconditions for learning that appear to have been necessary for organizational learning to take place. While such a discussion must necessarily be tentative, given the slender reed of theory and research on which it rests, it is well to attempt to summarize key aspects of what has been learned, if only to help frame the issues for those whose efforts in this area will come later.

The Preconditions for Learning

There are at least two broad approaches or umbrellas under which the discussion on preconditions for learning can proceed. One is to take the "policy cycle" as the frame of reference, examine how program and policy evaluations can contribute to organizational learning at each stage of the policy cycle. From this perspective, the emphasis is on the organizational need for information at different phases of the policy cycle and what does or does not facilitate the ability of the organization to obtain and learn from that information it requires.

The second approach would be to focus on the governmental decision-making process, addressing the issue of who sends/provides information within an organization, who receives/needs the information, the form and content of what is sent, and under what circumstances these various components all come together in a fashion that learning can occur. The emphasis here would be on the institutional actors and processes that are (or are not) in place and that serve as providers/filters/users of information relative to the governance of public sector organizations.

So as to maximize the opportunity for identifying the lessons from these cases, and recognizing that in comparative work, the implications from one approach may be more or less applicable to any individual country, both strategies will be followed. The discussion to follow will examine preconditions for learning suggested by the country cases and from each of these two vantage points.

The Policy Cycle

One vantage from which to read the preceding studies is to examine when it is in the life of an individual program or policy that information can be brought to bear that influences subsequent thinking and action by a governmental organization with respect to that policy or program (cf. Rist 1993). Stated differently, not all available information about a policy or program at all phases of its existence is relevant or necessary for organizational learning about that same policy or program. Information is content specific and is thus more or less relevant to potential users at different phases of the policy cycle.

Governmental decision making is multidimensional and multifaceted. The information generated by policy and program evaluation is but one among a number of frequently contradictory and competing sources of influence that come into play as a public sector organization continually adapts to its environment by redirecting resources, identifying new customers, reframing its vision, and balancing competing demands from many parts of the political arena. Decision making in this context is constantly evolving; it is a process of working through cycles of change in the life of a policy or program. Public sector decision making is thus a process with its own order and logic, its own time tables, pressures, and iterations.

To think of organizational learning in this context, and in light of the studies in this volume, the traditional understanding of decision making appears in need of substantial reformulation. In this traditional approach, decision making is understood as a discrete event, undertaken by a discrete set of actors, working in "real time," and moving toward a decision based on an analysis of the options. Organizational learning would be viewed, from this perspective, as occurring when that information necessary to enhance the decision-making capability and certainty of the key actors was both made available and subsequently utilized.

Policy-making is thus an event and organizational learning takes place when the decisions are made based on the use of new information, that is, new inputs generated new questions and new thinking on what to do. Whether the subsequent decision is single- or double-loop in nature is less the overriding issue than is the fact that when faced with a discrete decision-making event, information makes a difference. Weiss nicely summarizes this notion of "decision making as an event" (1982:23):

The Preconditions for Learning 195

Both the popular and the academic literature picture decision making as an event; a group of authorized decision makers assemble at particular times and places, review a problem (or opportunity), consider a number of alternative courses of action with more or less explicit calculation of the advantages and disadvantages of each option, weigh the alternatives against their goals or preferences, and then select an alternative that seems well suited to achieving their purposes. The result is a decision.

She also cleanly undercuts this view when she writes (1982:26):

Given the fragmentation of authority across multiple bureaus, departments, and legislative committees, and the disjointed stages by which actions coalesce into decisions, the traditional model of decision making is a highly stylized rendition of reality. Identification of any clear-cut group of decision makers can be difficult. (Sometimes a middle-level bureaucrat has taken the key action, although he or she may be unaware that his or her action was going to be—or was—decisive.) The goals of policy are often equally diffuse, except in terms of "taking care of" some undesirable situation. Which opinions are considered, and what set of advantages or disadvantages are assessed, may be impossible to tell in the interactive, multiparticipant, diffuse process of formulating policy. The complexity of governmental decision making often defies neat compartmentalization.

Thinking of organizational learning within this latter framework leads to some very different assumptions about learning than one would find with the former. Not the least of these is that with the latter, learning becomes part of an web of interacting forces, sources of information, power systems, and institutional arrangements. Organizational learning becomes part of an on-going process by which a governmental institution adapts. The learning occurring within a governmental system is hard to pinpoint. Even harder is trying to identify the particular decision or policy redirection that can be attributed to a uniquely self-contained source of data or information. This is exactly the engineering model of decision making that Weiss challenges in her quote above. Organizational learning is thus understood to be something quite other than the mastery of individual facts and data in order to sit and make a discrete decision.

The emphasis on the policy cycle as a framework for studying organizational learning establishes the means by which one can identify those potential linkages between the supply of policy relevant information and its use. Again, it is important to emphasize that we are addressing the issue of the preconditions for learning—not attempting to specify the precise instances, time frames, or places in the policy cycle where learning must necessarily occur. The emphasis is thus on what appears to be the positive preconditions under which organizational learning takes places within a governmental system and so allows that system to respond with new behaviors, whether single- or double-loop in nature.

The policy cycle as discussed here occurs in three phases—policy formulation, policy implementation, and policy accountability. Each of these three phases is distinct, has its own set of actors/decision makers involved, and has its own demands for information. The message from this present set of studies suggests that when phase-specific policy and program evaluation material are developed and made available to the appropriate decision makers at the appropriate time, a key precondition for learning has taken place. Having cycle-specific information available within the system, accessible to those involved in the deliberations, targeted to the issues being discussed, and trusted by those involved is not sufficient to ensure that learning will occur or that use will follow. But it is a necessary step if information is to be the source of learning within the organization.

What may at first glance seem a simplistic prescription for organizational learning (right data, right people, right time) is actually much more difficult than it appears. Here the thinking of Carol Weiss is helpful by describing decision making as a process rather than an event. The "right data" are seldom available, seldom packaged in such a way to be useful to decision makers, and seldom framed in ways that answer the particular policy cycle questions on the table. It is more frequent that data on policy implementation, for example, are available when what are needed are data on accountability. It is also more frequent that what data are available are incomplete, outmoded, and difficult to reanalyze in such a way as to be specific to the new questions at hand.

The same can be said for getting the material to the "right people" so that they can use it in their decision making. Weiss aptly notes that it is often questionable as to just who are the right people. Actors on the policy stage are constantly rewriting the script, switching roles, and leaving the play altogether. Therefore, the notion that there is a "right" person or group of persons for particular information is open to question. It may be more appropriate to think of getting the right information to the right cluster of policy actors (however ill-defined this may be), or into the right policy system rather than seeking out an individual to whom a report must be given. The latter happens constantly, and it is the model by which many in the policy arena operate, but getting the right report (however defined) to the right person (however defined) does not ensure that decisions will be made or use drawn from the material. Things are not always as they appear. The person who looks from the outside to be the "right person" for a report or analysis may be, in reality, far from the mark.

The same can be said for the right timing. Only in those cases when the researcher or policy analyst believes there will be a discrete decision made based on a discrete set of data can an argument be made for timing as a key aspect of organizational learning. Here the presumption flies in the face of experience. Most decisions are iterative, involve multiple actors, take place over time, cut across lines of authority and responsibility, and are constantly open to reexamination and revision. Decisions seldom, within government, stay made. (I am not sure they do stay made elsewhere, but because governance is the constant process of balancing demands, needs, and political pressures, decisions are most often temporary and partial, not permanent and complete.)

Having given the impression in these past paragraphs that public sector governance is little more than constant improvisation and ad hoc muddling through, I would hasten to note that the studies in this volume do speak of a different situation, of governments learning from the material supplied by policy and program evaluation. The point is not that learning is not taking place, but rather that it is taking place in more subtle and differentiated ways than the "decision making as event" analysts would posit. Recognizing the nature of the policy cycle and how it is that different information needs emerge at different phases of that cycle can greatly enhance the opportunities for organizational learning.

Examples of organizational learning found in the preceding studies where there is an explicit link to one or more phases of the policy cycle would include those from Belgium, The Netherlands, and the United States. The Dutch case addresses most directly policy implementation, the Belgium case that of policy accountability, and the United States case frames its analysis most closely to what we are terming policy formulation. Again, the point is that because there are distinct information needs at each phase of the policy cycle, evidence of organizational learning becomes apparent when relevant information appropriate to cycle-specific needs is used to generate either a single- or double-loop response.

The strength of the policy cycle approach to the study of organizational learning is that it provides a context by which the real information needs of government are linked to eventual behaviors that demonstrate learning coming from the fulfilling of these same information needs. It is also the case that this approach does not a priori assume that learning must always be present or that information will always be used. The approach treats organizational learning as a process that may or may not occur, and often not in the way or at the time when it would be anticipated.

Organizational learning is not, from this vantage, something that can be programmed or forced to occur. Frequently, policy decisions are weak, wrong, and counterproductive. These decisions may be the result of poor or too little information. Sometimes the information is good, but the system did not know how to absorb it. In still other instances, the information was correct, appropriately applied to the issue at hand, but other forces overrode the direction of the eventual governmental action.

Examining organizational learning from this perspective recognizes the reality of politics, the scarcity and incompleteness of necessary information, the multiple forces beyond information that influence decision making, and the fact that information relevant to one phase of the policy cycle may be totally inappropriate to another. Thus, the link between policy and program evaluation information on the one hand and organizational learning on the other has a basis in the practical realities of governing. Organizational learning cannot be taken for granted, nor can it be taken for granted that solid policy and program evaluation information will necessarily generate organizational learning. The learning may take place, and it may be influenced by policy and program evaluation. But then this is only one of the four possibilities of the two-by-two table one can generate when juxtaposing organizational learning against the presence of policy and program evaluation information.

The present set of studies indicate that learning does happen and happens across governments. But we are unable to discuss at this time the frequency, persistence, or extent of such learning within different governmental systems. Incidentally, the same must necessarily be said for other types of information available to governments. The existing research literature supplies no assurances that economic data, budgetary data, internal auditing data, or even national security data are used differently or more directly than what we have found here with policy and program evaluation information.

If the sequence for organization learning from within this framework were to be briefly summarized, it would unfold as follows: policymaking takes place within a policy arena where there are different information needs required for the successful management and steering at each of the three stages of the policy in question. For each stage of the policy cycle, policy and program evaluation information needs form a subset of all information needed by the policymakers for the management of the policy in question. If these particular information needs relevant to policy and program evaluation could be met, the resulting information could be of assistance to those responsible for governance. On some occasions, those information needs are more or less met and the information is of more or less assistance. In many other instances, the information needs are not met or are ignored and there is no reason to think further about the emergence of organizational learning around the topic at hand.

Within a subset of these occasions where cycle-specific information is available, the information becomes part of the discourse of those policymakers involved in steering or deciding a course of action. In still a smaller subset of the occasions when the information is discussed and actually influences governmental activity, it is permissible to say that organizational learning has occurred and that this learning is either single- or double-loop in nature. It is in these instances that we can speak of organizational learning being influenced by policy and program evaluation analysis.

Governmental Decision-Making Processes

Seeking to understand the preconditions for learning via the study of organizational decision making allows one to address issues of who are the decision makers, who are those who provide them with relevant policy and program evaluation information, what is the format in which the information is provided, and what is the content of the information. In short, here one can approach organizational learning from the vantage of communication styles, decision-making strategies, the values and beliefs of those in decision-making positions, and how receptive an organization is (or is not) to information that comes from within or from outside the organization itself.

One precondition for learning, based on the studies reported here, is that governmental organizations appear more receptive to information produced internally than that which comes from external sources. The chapters by Sonnichsen and by Mayne both strongly suggest that the credibility of the material is greater if the recipients know it has come from within their own organization. The proclivity to give greater reliance and trust to information generated from within allows this information through the various filters any organization sets up as it comes to accept some information as worthy of attention and reaction and other material as irrelevant. These two chapters would suggest that the filters are more effective (and deliberately so) in keeping information from outside the organization to a minimum. Sonnichsen's chapter on internal evaluation and audit groups in particular suggests they are in a position to have their information reach the very highest levels of their organizations—and thus are more likely to have it read and attended to by those in position of authority.

No organization, one might generalize, likes bad news about itself. But if there is bad new to be given, better it come from within than from without. And if this bad news necessitates an organizational response, better the organization be in a position to say that they are proactively taking care of their own problems than that they are reacting to negative news from elsewhere. I make a point here of stressing "bad news" because negative information can be just as much a catalyst for learning as is positive information. Organizations, like individuals, can learn from their mistakes. But the manner in which the mistake is discovered and how it is portrayed within the organization has a great influence on the willingness of the organization to admit to having made the mistake and being willing to rectify it.

A second precondition for learning, and this builds on the first, is that there appears to be a positive correlation between the credibility of the source and the acceptance of the information. Information that comes into an organization from an outside organization that is not seen to be legitimate, or information that comes into an organization without a legitimate inside sponsor is information that is not likely to be accepted and acted upon. Governmental organizations appear to be clearly antagonistic to the information often provided by whistle-blowers, to the charges of some special interest groups, to calls for organizational reform, and to allegations of poor performance. Information that comes into the organization in this way is more likely to be negated and rebutted than to be accepted.

The reverse also seems to hold true according to the cases presented here. An organization will accept outside information when the source appears credible, nonconfrontational, and the benefits for the receiving organization are evident. The GAO study of OPM is one such instance where positive outcomes were evident from the efforts of GAO to work with OPM to improve OPM's management communication systems. Likewise, the evaluation of the Belgium post office and the subsequent receptivity of the Belgium postal officials to the information from the study suggests that they viewed the source of the study in a positive light and were interested in the findings—especially given that they had no comparable data of their own.

A third precondition for learning highlighted here is that organizational learning is not only dependent upon how the organization perceives the supplier of the information (note also the Canadian example in this regard), but also on how the organization perceives the internal receiver. If the internal receiver of the information is credible and speaks on behalf of the information coming from outside, the receptivity will be greater. If the receiver is marginal to the organization, has little credibility, and has little access to those with decision-making responsibility, then the likelihood of that external information finding its way into the deliberations of the organization are nearly nil.

A fourth precondition for public sector learning involves the legitimacy of interinstitutional scrunity. This is an increasingly important dimension to governmental activity as there are governmental organizations whose sole purpose is to maintain oversight of other governmental organizations. The GAO in the United States, the auditor general in Canada, the Court of Audit in the Netherlands, and the National Audit Office in Sweden are but four examples where oversight of other government agencies is a prime if not sole responsibility.

The kinds of information developed in these organizations and shared with other sectors of the government can have a significant impact on the subsequent behavior of the affected organizational units. While one might venture that most of the studied organizations will respond with single-loop learning ("You told us about a problem and we have taken care of it"), there is the possibility of double-loop learning as well—especially if the two organizations have developed a working relationship over time. Here the GAO and OPM example comes to mind. The authority of some governmental institutions to force compliance and change in other institutions can generate a real, if begrudging learning.

A fifth precondition for organizational learning involves the medium by which the information is shared with the relevant institution. Informal contact and a strategy of "no surprises" establishes the level of interpersonal communication and trust necessary for the recipients of new information to incorporate that information into the organization. While the national studies from Sweden, Canada, and the Netherlands all indicate that organizational learning did occur, it is not clear from those studies how it was that the information was conveyed beyond (if at all) the formal issuing of a report. In each of these three instances, the studies documented that governmental officials did suggest that the formal reports had an impact. But what is unknown is the context, the political and organizational receptivity, and whether individual actors within the systems were open to the conveyance of the information.

The institutional case studies, on the other hand, do show that the building of contact, trust, and channels of communication all impacted upon the acceptance of the information. This was the case whether the source of the information was external to the organization (the Belgium evaluation and the GAO evaluation) or developed from within (the internal evaluation offices in the FBI and elsewhere). The point here is that it is hard to document any instance where a report, simply by itself, generated organizational learning. It would be surprising if this were so, for all we have learned in these studies suggests that context, contacts, and credibility are vital to any organization opening itself up to new information. Beyond that, for an organization to act upon any information with the intent of seeking to improve itself requires an alignment of so many variables that making the argument for a report having an impact directly upon the learning of an organization is highly unlikely.

It is not known from the studies reported here how institutions respond to the formal transmittal of information via reports, testimonies, press coverage, and so on. Which of these vehicles is more or less effective than another in gaining acceptance within an organization for the information is a question still to be explored. Here again, it appears from what information we do have that the source of the information is highly relevant as is the context in which that information is shared and how widely the information is known. Wide press coverage of an event where it is perceived that government did not respond appropriately is likely to generate considerable attention and reaction on the part of that same governmental organization. Learning how to ensure that the same response does not occur again and generate still more negative public reaction is likely to be of high priority to the managers of that organization. The learning may be single-loop in nature, but there is some assurance that the status quo will not hold.

The final precondition for learning that may be posited, based on the studies reported here, is that the efforts to generate learning within an organization have no conclusion. There is no finish line. The context continually changes, the actors switch roles, the interest of the press moves elsewhere, the information that was crucial and highly topical at one time is irrelevant at another, and credibility of both the source and content has to be constantly renewed. Nothing with respect to organizational learning stays still for very long. The half-life of the entire process is very short. Starting over is a given.

Conclusions

Those in the policy and program evaluation communities who are interested in the improvement of government and seek to have the information they generate understood and become influential had better commit themselves for the long term. What the studies reported here suggest is that the promise of public sector learning can be fulfilled, but that it cannot be taken for granted. Change is a given. Further, chance is a given. Much has to be right for an organization to learn. But much can go wrong and then little happens. The organization perpetuates its old ways of behaving, no new information enters the system, and the system moves along until it is again confronted with the challenge/opportunity to think about itself differently. The presence of policy and program evaluation information has been established in these studies to influence organizational learning. But for the efforts to be more than episodic and erratic, a sustained commitment to producing useful information and working with the users of such information is an imperative.

The concept of organizational learning used for our work has remained surprisingly robust and intact throughout our efforts. This was not at all to be assumed when we began. The comparative information on organizational learning is quite slim, and the applications to the public sector are slimmer still. What the current studies suggest is that there is merit in the concept and that further work could be fruitfully undertaken to explore and expand upon what has been found in this present effort.

Conducting comparative research is precarious, difficult, and time consuming. Without the vitality of the intellectual questions, the commitment of the individual researchers, and the interest in working with a set of international colleagues, the ability to sustain the time and effort in collaborative undertakings such as this is tenuous. That this present study has been completed speaks to each of the necessary ingredients—an intriguing intellectual question, the commitment of the researchers to see their individual studies through to completion, and the interest in being part of an international network of academic and government officials working collaboratively to generate innovative research on a topic that impacts upon every government in existence. Success has come with the opportunity to learn. The lesson for an organization is much the same, even if the particulars are different. Learning generates success.

References

Blankenhage, E. E. 1992. "An Historical Study of Organizational Learning in the Development of Doctrine in the U.S. Army, 1979–1986." Ph.D. diss., George Washington University.

Chelimsky, E. 1991. "On the Social Science Contribution to Governmental Decision-Making." *Science* 254 (October).

Duncan, R., and A. Weiss. 1979. "Organizational Learning: Implications for Organizational Design." In *Research in Organizational Behavior,* ed. B. Shaw. Greenwich, CT: JAI Press.

Galagan, P. 1989. "Growth: Mapping Its Patterns and Periods." *Training and Development Journal* 11.

Normann, R. 1985. "Developing Capabilities for Organizational Learning." In *Organizational Strategy and Change,* ed. J. M. Pennings and Associates. San Francisco: Jossey-Bass Publishers.

Rist, R. C. 1993. "Influencing the Policy Process with Qualitative Research." In *Handbook of Qualitative Research,* ed. N. Denzin, and Y. Lincoln. Newbury Park, CA: Sage Publications.

Stata, R. 1989. "Organizational Learning—The Key to Management Innovation." *Sloan Management Review* (Spring).

Weiss, C. 1982. "Policy Research in the Context of Diffuse Decision Making." In *Policy Studies Review Annual,* vol. 6, ed. R. C. Rist. Newbury Park, CA: Sage Publications.

Contributors

MARIE LOUISE BEMELMANS-VIDEC is head of the Division for Quality Evaluation, The Netherlands Court of Audit, The Hague and professor of public administration at the Catholic University of Nijmegen. She was a Senior Fulbright Fellow in the United States in 1988. She is widely published on evaluation utilization and human resource management issues in The Netherlands. She is co-editor of *Advancing Public Policy Evaluation* and a forthcoming book on the linkage of policy evaluation and policy instruments. Dr. Bemelmans-Videc is a founding member of the IIAS Working Group.

BJARNE ERIKSEN was, until his retirement in 1993, the assistant director general of the Directorate of Public Management for the Norwegian government. He has published on the committee structure of NATO, the role of evaluation in public sector management, and human resource management. He has been a strong advocate for the introduction of program evaluation in the Norwegian government. Mr. Eriksen is a founding member of the IIAS Working Group.

JAN-ERIC FURUBO is the head of the Division for Results Based Management, Evaluation, and Budgetary Questions in the National Audit Bureau of Sweden and the author of books and articles in the fields of evaluation and budgeting. A central focus of his writings has been the study of the effects of information campaigns and other policy instruments in areas such as energy conservation and health policy.

EDIE GOLDENBERG is dean of the College of Literature, Science, and the Arts and at the University of Michigan in Ann Arbor and a member of the National Academy of Public Administration. She has published widely in the areas of the relationship between the media and public affairs, political campaigns and election analyses, civil service reform, and press portrayals of the gender gap.

FRANS LEEUW is currently the director of the Department of Policy Evaluation at the Netherlands Court of Audit, The Hague and a professor at Utrecht University in the Department of Sociology, where he teaches on policy effectiveness research. He was a Senior Fulbright Fellow in the United States in 1981, has published widely on program evaluation, policy research methods, performance auditing, and evaluation utilization, and is co-editor of the book, *What Has Dutch Sociology Achieved?*

JOHN LEITCH is an assistant director with the General Government Division of the United States General Accounting Office in Washington D.C. He has conducted numerous studies for the GAO over the past twenty years on organizational change, performance and productivity management, and government-wide reorganization, quality, and productivity programs.

FABIENNE LELOUP is currently a lecturer in the Department of Political Science and Public Administration at the Catholic University Faculties of Mons, Belgium. Her fields of research are applied to public management questions and to the study of developing countries.

JOHN MAYNE is manager of the Services Standards Initiative for the Treasury Board Secretariat within the Canadian government. He formerly held the position as director, evaluation policy, Office of the Comptroller General, in Ottawa. He served as president of the Canadian Evaluation Society from 1985 to 1987. Has published numerous articles on program evaluation, policy analysis, and performance measurement, and is co-editor of *Advancing Public Policy Evaluation* and a forthcoming book on the linkage of evaluation and performance measurement.

RAY C. RIST is professor of educational leadership and director of the Center for Policy Studies at The George Washington University in Washington, D.C. He has held senior government positions in both the legislative and executive branches of the U.S. government and has had previous academic appointments at The Johns Hopkins University and

Cornell University. He has authored or edited eighteen books and more than 100 articles. He was a Senior Fulbright Fellow at the Max Planck Institute in Germany from 1976 to 1977. Dr. Rist is a founding member of the IIAS Working Group.

PIET ROZENDAL directs a unit within the Netherlands Court of Audit that addresses performance auditing and value-for-money studies. He has held prior positions in both the academic and private sectors managing program evaluation studies. His academic training is in social and organizational psychology.

RICHARD SONNICHSEN is a private consultant whose main interests and numerous publications are in the areas of the development and functioning of internal organizational program evaluation units and in the utilization of evaluation results. In 1993 he retired as deputy assistant director in change of the Office of Planning, Evaluation, and Audits at the Federal Bureau of Investigation. Dr. Sonnichsen is also an adjunct professor at the University of Southern California, Washington Public Affairs Center.

PHILIPPE SPAEY is head of the Department of Political Sciences and Public Administration at the Catholic University Faculties of Mons, Belgium where he teaches political science and comparative politics. He is presently in the midst of a long-term program evaluation study of the modernization and restructuring of the Belgium postal system. Preliminary results from this evaluation have been reported at recent meetings of the American Evaluation Association and the Canadian Evaluation Society.

Index

Belgium Postal System: corporate culture in, 113–114, 121; customers, 113; deterioration of, 107; independent public company, 110–111; organization, 111–113; restructuring, 108, 120.
Bureau of Land Management (USA), 134.

Canada: Auditor General, 201; Office of the Comptroller General, 21, 22, 23, 25, 28; evaluation, expectations of use, 26–27, factors affecting use 29–34, institutionalization of, 22; organizational impact of, 28, scope in federal government, 23, supply/demand model, 17, 35–40, utilization in federal government, 117, 21, 24–26, 28–29.

Department of Health and Human Services (USA), 133–134.
Decision making: rational model, 1–2; processes for, 199–203.

Evaluation: formative approach, 109; links to budgeting and auditing, 181, 191; links to organizational learning, 10, 192–203; management of, 68–70; model forms of, 147; organizational integration of, 8–9; program use of, 19; supply/demand model of utilization, 17, 35–40; two-wave theory in national development, 149–150, 178–181; use by organizations, 11, 17, 19–20, 125–127.

Federal Bureau of Investigation (FBI), (USA), 133, 202.

General Accounting Office (GAO) (USA), 89–90, 201, 202; organizational functions, 93; performance evaluations, 94.

Human Resources Management: Canada, 155–159, 178; France, 174–177, 179; Germany, 159–162, 178; Great Britain, 170–174, 179; The Netherlands, 162–166, 178; Scandinavian countries, 166–170, 179; strategic management of, 145; socialization and sanction functions, 147–149, 180; United States of America, 150–155, 178; use of program evaluation in, 146, 178–180.

Netherlands, The: Court of Audit, 71, 83, 201; policy evaluations, in central government, 71–74, management provisions for, 74–75, utilization of, 75–80.

Office of Personnel Management (OPM) (USA): organization of, 91–93; organizational learning within, 103–104, 201, 202; performance evaluation structure, 90, 95–97; self evaluation, 98; utilization of GAO evaluations, 101–103, 201; utilization of performance evaluations, 98–101.
Organizational evaluation: influence of decision-making process, 127; and internal evaluation units, 18, 126–129, characteristics of effectiveness, 21, 130–133, models for, 135–139; receptivity to, 200; use of findings, 127.
Organization learning: and accountabil-

211

ity, 7–8; credibility of source, 200–201; decision-making process, 199–203; definition of, 3, 89–90, 189; double-loop, 3, 5, 10, 18, 23, 25, 38–40, 56–58, 61–63, 69, 80–82, 90, 100, 104, 122, 133, 145, 191; evaluation research on, 4–6; and policy cycle, 194–199; private sector, 191–192; public sector, 189–193; single-loop, 3, 5, 10, 18, 20, 25, 38–40, 59, 61–63, 69, 80–82, 90, 104, 121, 133, 145, 191; structure required, 95, 139–140; theoretical basis for, 2–4, 94; utilization of evaluation research in, 68–69, 126–127, 193–203.

Sweden: budget process, 47, 51–53; decision-making processes within government, agency decision-making, 53–55, budget process, 51–53, 59–60, fundamental policy decisions, 48–51, 62, impacts on policy makers, 56–59; evaluation infrastructure, 62; National Audit Bureau, 56, 201; structure of public administration, 45–47.

Utilization of Evaluation: art of judgement, 146–147; context for use, 78; credibility of, 33–34; decision-making process, 48–62; enlightenment function, 18; evidence of use, 78–80; factors affecting use, 29–34; measurement problems, 20–21, 84; organizational use, 19–20, 30; policy cycle, 18, 194–199; process factors, 30–33; program use, conceptual,.19, 24, 28, instrumental, 19, 24, 28, 75–80; supply/demand model of, 17, 35–40.

The International Institute of Administrative Sciences and Its Working Group on Policy and Program Evaluation

The International Institute of Administrative Sciences (IIAS) is a scientific institution, whose vocation is international, specializing in public administration and the administrative sciences. Its field covers all questions which concern contemporary public administration at the national and international levels. Imagined already as early as 1910 by administrators and politicians and established in 1930 by the International Congress of Administrative Sciences held in Madrid, the IIAS is the first of the specialized institutions to affirm, worldwide, its scientific willingness to resolve the problems and challenges of national and international administration.

The purpose of the IIAS is to promote the development of administrative sciences, the better operation of public administrative agencies, the improvement of administrative methods and technics and the progress of international administration. Its history demonstrates its capacity to respond to the needs of the industrialized and developing countries, as well as to those in transition. Owing to its attributes and great experience, the IIAS is a unique organization which is comprised of 48 Member States, 9 Governmental International Organizations, 49 National Sections and 54 Corporate Members.

A large part of IIAS activities is devoted to information (IIAS publications, its quarterly International Review of Administrative Sciences, published in French and English, and its information and documentation service attached to its Library) and to expertise and consultancy. The Institute responds to specific requests of governments, international organizations or any other agency. But most IIAS research activities are carried out in the framework of its annual major meetings (Congress, Conference or Round Table) and its Working Groups (12 currently).

One of these Working Groups, and one of the most productive, was launched in 1986 and, since this date, has been working on Policy and Program Evaluation. Since its beginning, the Dr. Ray C. Rist has presided, the group which is now comprised of more than 35 members from 16 countries. The group meets once a year and, in the framework of sub-groups, prepares books which present the findings of their intensive research. The latest book, *"Can Governments Learn?"*, presents the efforts of one of these sub-groups.

IIAS, rue Defacqz 1 box 11, B–1050 BRUXELLES, BELGIQUE